Google Classroom for Teachers :

The Complete Guide for Teachers on How to Teach Using Google Classroom and to Benefit From Virtual Learning

Katy F. Olson

Table of Contents

Introduction

Congratulations on purchasing *Google Classroom for Teachers: The Complete Step-By-Step Illustrated Guide for Teachers on How to Teach Using Google Classroom and to benefit From Virtual Learning,* and thank you for doing so.

The following chapters will discuss virtual learning and how Google Classroom will make this the best experience possible. You are a teacher, and you became a teacher so that you could use your knowledge to help other people navigate the world of learning. But a changing world mandates the use of more online learning and less face-to-face time, which means that the virtual learning processes of Google Classroom are just what you need to streamline your life.

From communicating with your students to grading their assignments and providing feedback, Google Classroom gives you all of the tools you need to implement virtual learning for your students. In an easy-to-use format with numerous applications created to make your job easier, Google Classroom is the system that all teachers need. Teachers today face challenges and opportunities that have never been seen before in the world of education. Some incredible benefits are waiting for the virtual teacher, and using Google Classroom is the best method for reaching students in the best possible way. This fantastic application lets teachers spend their time doing what they do best, and that is teaching.

There are plenty of books on this subject on the market; thanks again for choosing this one! Every effort was made to ensure it is full of as much useful information as possible; please enjoy!

Chapter 1: Google Classroom for Teachers

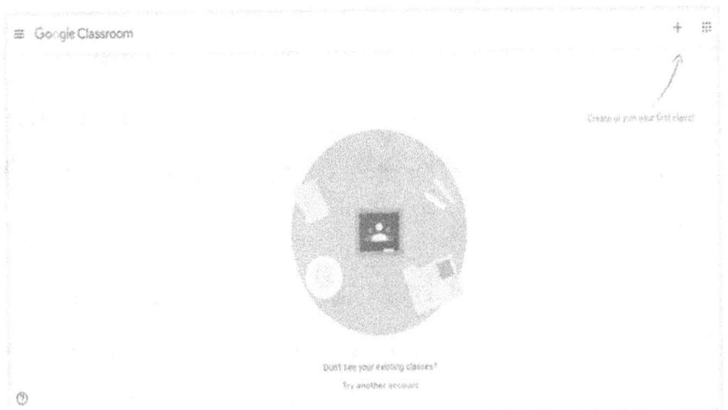

Google Classroom is an innovative web service that Google developed for schools to simplify the creation, distribution, and grading of assignments. The ultimate purpose of Google Classroom is to make the process of sharing files between students and their teachers more streamlined.

The site has created a cohesive platform that integrates a calendar, Gmail, slides, sheets, and docs to enable teachers to manage communication with their students in a virtual learning environment. Within the system, teachers can manage assignments and broadcast a class calendar. Each class that the teacher is overseeing can be organized in their file folder on Google Classroom. This folder allows students to complete their work and then submit their assignments to the teacher. The calendar can be edited to adjust for due dates and tasks. The teacher can monitor the progress of the student by keeping track of when and how often the assignment is accessed by the student who is working on it. The teacher will track the revision history of each document, and after completion, they can grade the class work and return them to the students with appropriate comments attached.

While Google Classroom is specifically designed to be used by teachers for teaching their classes virtually, the idea was born from an earlier service known as Google G Suite. That was a site that Google implemented in the first part of the twenty-first century to allow people to share documents, access their email, store information and files, and collaborate with other users. The site came complete with a virtual meeting room, a calendar function, and a multipurpose feature called Google Hangouts, which took the place of several other Google communication features. Hangouts offer clients the ability to chat with one another electronically or verbally, and the opportunity to conduct videoconferencing with other people. This service proved to be particularly useful as the business world expanded into the global market, and more people began working from home instead of commuting to the office. The services of G Suite are free for consumers to use, although it does offer optional upgraded business-related products for a fee.

With the success of Google G Suite, the decision was made to create an online platform that would be the ultimate location for classroom teachers who needed to connect with students over the internet via home computers. In 2014 Google Classroom debuted with a preview that was made available to some of the current users of Google's G

Suite for Education services. In 2017 Google Classroom was made available to all users whether they subscribed to G Suite for Education or not. Later in the year, Google allowed any Google user to create and teach a virtual class using the services of Google Classroom. In 2018 the classroom was refreshed to allow teachers the ability to organize classroom content by topic, improved the grading interface, added a section for classwork, and allowed classwork to be reused for other classes. In 2019 they added the ability to add assignments into the classwork section. The best added on feature probably came in 2020 when Google set up a better system of integration with Google Meet, which allowed teachers to have a unique link for meeting within each class. Google Meet is the updated name for Google Hangouts, and it is a service that was developed by Google for video communications.

Technical Features of Google Classroom

Google Classroom has all of the necessary features to enable teachers and educational institutions to move to a paperless system if they want. It ties together many of the best Google features to allow for a wholly integrated experience for students and teachers.

Google Drive is the synchronization and file storage service provided by Google. It allows users to synchronize files across more than one server, store files, and share files. The file storage feature will enable users of the site to upload files to a central location that will be accessed by other users who have permission to use those files. File sharing is the practice of providing access to and distributing different digital media. This sharing can include electronic books or music, documents, multimedia, or computer programs. The most common methods being used are computer networks, where many different users are part of one group of users, using removable media to share files, and using systems to distribute files to other users. File synchronization is essential because it will allow the shared and stored files to receive updates no matter where they are when specific rules are followed. This updating is done by setting a parameter for the file and the information that needs to be updated. For example, if users were all sharing a file about sales figures, the file could be set to update at a particular time of day with the current sales figures. This ability to update information would allow all users access to updated information when they open the file, every time they open the file, no matter where they are physically located.

Google Docs is an application that offers free spreadsheets and documents online that users can create, edit, and then stored online. Anyone can gain access to the files from any computer as long as they have internet access. When using Google Docs, the user can create spreadsheets and documents, and then edit them and update them as needed. There are various types of fonts and different formats for the individual files, as well as the ability to add images, tables, lists, and formulas to plain text. The program is compatible with most of the word processor applications and presentation software that is currently available on the market. The user can publish their work either as a manuscript ready for printing or a web page. The user will retain control over who can see and access their document. Google Docs is an ideal application for those who want to compose documents and spreadsheets for the general public to view and download, creating and maintaining personal or organizational blogs, or for creating and publishing work within the organization. One of the innovative features of Google Docs is that more than one person can work on a document together while in remote locations, and they can do this in real-time. The participants are all able to see what changes were made when they were made, and who made them. Google Sheets is the online spreadsheet application, and Google Slides is the online visual presentation application.

Gmail is one of the free online email services that users can access their personal and corporate email needs. Gmail was developed and is operated by Google. Users of this email service can assess Gmail from any web browser and on any computer or mobile device. They can also utilize third-party programs that are used to synchronize email content to retrieve emails. Users of Gmail can send emails that are as large as twenty-five megabytes, and they can receive emails that are up to fifty megabytes, including any attachments. They can also insert files from Google Drive into the message if they need to send larger files or emails. Gmail offers the ability to use a search orientation that allows the user to search the internet for information based on a particular query. It also provides emails in a conversational view, where the system recognizes that specific messages are related by group or subject. Google will then bring these emails together in one collection and stack them in a chain, one after the other, so that the messages look like a text conversation and the newest messages appear displayed at the top of the list.

Google Calendar is a scheduling and time-management service that was developed by Google and added to its product offering in general release in 2009. The calendar allows users to create events on the calendar and edit them later if needed. Users can enable a reminder for any occasion, and they can also include the location of the event and the time and type of event it is. Users can be invited to other events based on their preferences. Users are also able to disable or enable the internet visibility of unique calendars, including birthdays and holidays. Google will automatically retrieve the user's birth dates from their persona information and will display birthday cards on the appropriate day. Google will also display the dates of holidays and other special occasions that are specific to the region or country. Google Calendar also offers several added features like Events, where the event information from the user's email messages is automatically added to their calendar,

Reminders allows users to add information on must-do activities to their calendars, Smart Suggestions automatically adds in recommendations for locations and contacts based on the user's past preferences. Goals will let the user enter the information of a specific personal plan, and the calendar will remind the user of the activity at optimal times.

Classroom Assignments allow collaboration between students and between the teacher and the student. The assignments are stored on Google Classroom and are graded there also. The student will submit their projects to their Drive, and these documents are submitted for grading. This collaboration eliminates the need for continually sharing documents between the student and the teacher, which helps to streamline the process. The teacher can choose a particular file to use as a template, giving every student in the class the opportunity to edit their copy and submit it for grading instead of viewing, copying, and editing the same document. When the teacher specifies the need, the students can attach additional documents from their Drive to a specific assignment.

Google Classroom offers teachers several different methods for grading assignments. They can attach files to a project, allowing the student to get and edit an individual copy or view it. If the student is creating the file, they can make the file and then attach it to an assignment. The teachers have the option to monitor the progress of assignments while they are being worked on, so they can offer comments, and the student can edit the document. Once projects are submitted, they are graded by the teacher and returned to the student with comments. This allows the student to make revisions and resubmit the assignment. Once the assignment is graded, it can only be edited by the teacher unless the teacher asks the student explicitly for corrections to the assignment.

In the Communication feature in Google Classroom, teachers can post announcements to the classroom stream, and then the students can make comments. This feature allows for two-way communication between the students and the teachers. While students can post messages to the classroom stream, the messages posted by the teachers will always have priority. Student messages can also be moderated by the teacher. Students and teachers can use multiple types of social media, such as files from Google Drive or videos from YouTube, to share content to attach to announcements. The teacher can send emails to one or more students in the classroom stream using Gmail. All participants can access the communication feature online or on the mobile app.

The Originality Report allows students and teachers to see the sections or parts of submitted assignments that are an exact match or contain wording that is similar to another source on the internet. A feature for students lets them improve their writing by flagging content that is missing citations and highlighting source material to make acknowledging borrowed original work much more manageable. Teachers can use the Originality Report to view the integrity of the work submitted by the student. The report will check the student's submission against billions of books and web pages using a single keystroke. The system will then highlight links to external sources and potential plagiarism in the assignment. The student can check their work three times for the recommended citation before they submit the assignment. It will also help them properly incorporate outside ideas into their work and show them how to build on these ideas. Teachers are also able to compare the work of one student to another within the system using the work of current and previous students from the information filed in the system.

At the end of the term or the year, the teacher can archive the course to keep their current classes more organized. The archived content is placed in file storage when it is removed from the homepage of the classroom. Archived class content can be viewed by teachers and students, but it can't be edited unless it is restored by the teacher. Google Classroom is available for download as a mobile app for both IOS and Android devices. The mobile app will allow users to access the content offline, share files from other apps into the classroom content, and take photos and attach them to the classroom content. Google Classroom never shows advertisements in any of its products, and the content of the users is never used for advertising purposes or scanned for any purpose.

The Modern Virtual Teacher

Until recently, most teachers, students, and school districts were neither prepared for nor experienced with teaching classes remotely in a virtual setting. Worldly events mandated the use of virtual teaching. Whether or not these conditions will continue will depend on many different factors. Some larger school districts are planning to incorporate virtual learning into their regular offering for students. Residents in rural areas may not have this freedom of choice due to the lack of reliable internet service.

Besides the disparities in the availability of technology, there are also differences in the abilities of teachers to teach virtual learning. Virtual classroom experiences demand that the teacher provide virtual instructions to the students, teach them new assignments, and be able to access the progress of the students continuously. The ability to teach effectively while teaching online classes depends significantly on the power of the individual teacher to navigate online resources and prepare the material. More than just a few days' worth of preparation is needed to teach a class online. This preparation becomes even more evident as the student progresses higher through the levels of schooling. Where it might be relatively easy to teach the alphabet or necessary math skills to kindergarteners, teaching physics or chemistry in a virtual setting is more complicated.

There is also the fact that colleges and universities taught their students, future teachers how to teach in front of a classroom and not in front of a computer monitor. A large part of the effectiveness of classroom learning is the visual aids that teachers use to decorate their rooms with, something that might be lacking or nonexistent with online learning. Interaction between the teacher and the students, or between students, is not impossible online, but it does not give the immediate reaction that it would in the classroom. The rules that guide in-person instruction don't entirely apply to the online situation. The teachers will need to learn new strategies for teaching the students and new tools for teaching them.

One of the most significant negatives that many teachers see with online learning is the inability for the students to interact well with other students and for the teachers to develop meaningful relationships with their students. There is also the dilemma in deciding which content can be assigned for students to learn and practice on their own as assignments, and which content needs to be presented as live instruction. Online virtual learning does not need to be an experience full of negativity. There are many advantages to online learning that can be utilized for the benefit of teachers and students alike.

Instead of focusing on the isolation of students in the virtual setting, it is better to visualize communities of classrooms where students can learn with their peers and from their peers. In a location that has several schools on the same level, like two or more high schools, classes can be adapted to allow students from several schools to participate in the same online course. This option will give each student more personal resources, as well as feedback from people who live in situations that might be vastly different from theirs. It increases the possible applications for students to learn and to demonstrate that learning. Using online learning also allows for educators to teach and display the technological skills that are much in demand in today's world.

There are opportunities for virtual learning that allow for exploration and collaboration between students. Students can connect with other students in ways that are more interesting and more meaningful. Imagine a student in sunny California and a student in wintery Minnesota trading weather-related videos and experiences. Or think about the possibility of learning French or German culture by communicating with a student from France or Germany. The possibilities for learning are endless. Experiences like these will allow students to connect in more meaningful ways. They can also make connections with mentors and teachers who will ignite their interest and can foster the relationships that will support the interest of the students in other areas, helping to build their confidence and engagement level.

Blended and virtual classrooms will provide access to a large variety of online resources. Teachers can use these resources to educate students in a variety of different ways. They can also instruct students in ways to assimilate and use and not just gather and store the information that is available to them. A diverse society will require today's students to be various thinkers and players. Teachers can easily use online learning resources to teach new languages. This resource will work not just for those students who desire to learn an international language, but also for international students who are facing a language barrier in their new learning environment. Modern technology can assist in the advancement of students who might be left behind in the traditional classroom setting since virtual learning offers learning geared to individual styles as well as learning in different modalities. This option is essential for students with interrupted education, learning disabilities, or limited language proficiencies.

Virtual learning offers opportunities for teachers and school districts, as well. They can provide expanded access to educational resources for the students. Analyzing data will allow the schools to understand gaps in student's abilities and learning styles and create plans to close those gaps. Since the teachers will be able to monitor the student's progress along the way, they will be able to address deficiencies almost immediately. The student will benefit from continual feedback. The student can be part of the learning community while learning at their own pace. Teachers can offer virtual field trips to online learners so that the classroom field trip can take the students anywhere in the world. Using audio services and webcam, the teacher and student can conduct personal meetings, which will allow the student the opportunity to practice a skill with the teacher.

Individual teachers will need to make specific preparations before beginning to teach their virtual classes, just as they would make preparations in the traditional classroom. Their first preparation needs to be the space they are using for the school in their home. While a separate office is always pleasant, it is not required, as long as there is a space the teacher can dedicate to the classroom. This space will help them remain focused and productive while they are in the classroom. If they have invested in a webcam, then the proper dress is mandatory. However, the teacher decides to set up their space is entirely at their discretion, but it needs to look professional to mark the fact that this is time for school. And the teacher must ensure their equipment works before classes begin. It is a good idea to conduct audio and video tests on any equipment the teacher are using in advance of the first day of school. It is also a good idea to practice a few classes before recording them or going live with the production. All of these steps will minimize distractions and interruptions throughout the classroom experience.

The teacher will need to set clear expectations and guidelines for the virtual classroom, just as they do in the physical classroom. Besides basic housekeeping rules, there needs to be instruction for digital expectations. Recording a session between the student and teacher might be okay for the student to do, but recording other people in a classroom setting might be considered an invasion of their privacy. Teachers will need to instruct students in internet etiquette as well as classroom etiquette, to ensure that everyone is on the same page. This precaution will foster productive learning environments as well as giving the students ownership of their learning and their contribution to the class.

Communication is vital to the success of virtual learning. Students and teachers need to have open lines of communication, and this might be even more critical in the virtual classroom. Teachers need a method to communicate with parents and guardians regarding the student's progress or upcoming school news. This communication will also allow the teachers the opportunity to assess the student's emotional and social environments and ensure any needs are being addressed. Teachers and school systems can make phone calls and texts, send emails, schedule individual conferences, and post messages online to keep everyone involved informed and engaged.

Another key to the success of virtual learning is the ability to adapt and improve. Schools and teachers will need to continually gather feedback from their students and families to identify areas that need improvement. Educators can use online survey services to gather information from the students regarding their experiences in the classroom. They can also collect information about when the students are completing their work and how long they are spending on each assignment. This ability can help educators address how lessons are presented, as well as identifying any possible gaps between the teaching style and the learning of the student.

One of the most essential considerations for virtual educators to remember is that they are still a vital part of the student's life. Some students may not adjust well to the change in routine and procedure. The teacher and other students might be their only human contact for hours at a time. The teacher and the virtual learning will need to remain as constant as possible to ensure a good experience for each student. The teachers may need to develop new routines and new methods of communication. The virtual experience will change and adapt, and the teachers and students will be the authors of that change.

The Advantages of Google Classroom

With Google Classroom, the teacher can be part of a classroom that allows them to communicate with their students, give them constructive feedback when it is needed, and enjoy the ease of sharing assignments and documents with others. Google's addition to online education strives to make classrooms more effective and more interactive, as well as paperless. It is a blended learning platform that is free to use with a wide variety of benefits for both teachers and students. Google Classroom will take workflow management to the next level while it elevates the productivity of the classroom.

Google Classroom is easy to operate, and it is accessible from any device. Even those who do not use Google will be able to use Google Classroom. The site is delivered using the Google Chrome browser, so it is accessible from all tablets, mobile phones, and computers. Adding additional users, as many as you want, is easy to do, as well as utilizing the other features of Google Classroom. You can attach files from Google Drive, add links, post videos from YouTube, make announcements, and manage assignments.

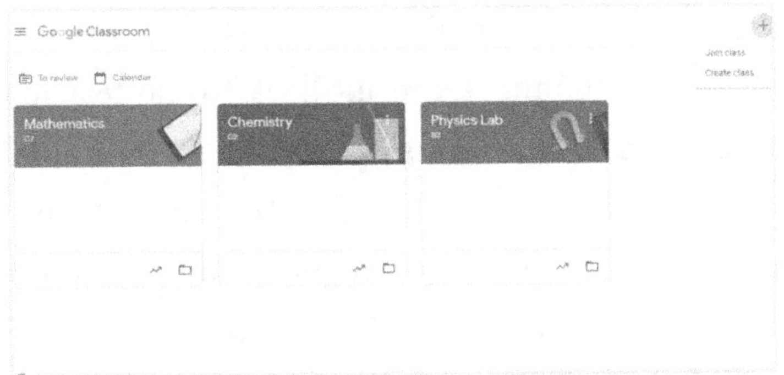

Google Docs is one of the best advantages of Google Classroom. Assignments or announcements created in Google Docs are saved online and can be shared with an infinite amount of people. If the document is shared, it will be able to be accessed immediately through Google Drive. Users of Google Docs can also personalize their files and organize them into folders in Google Drive. This option eliminates the need to send massive amounts of emails to impart information. All the user will need to do is create a document and share it with users to share information.

It is easier to create the assignments and then shares them with students in Google Classroom. Once the work is completed, it is just as easy for the student to submit the result back to the teacher. Processing assignments is more effective and much faster with Google Docs. Teachers can also see immediately who has completed and submitted their studies and who is still working on them and might need assistance. Teachers can offer immediate feedback to those who need it. And since the input can be given immediately, it will be more useful for the students and their learning process.

Google Classroom promotes paperless learning! Within Google Classroom, teachers can use eLearning materials that are centrally located in one location that is based in the cloud. This gives the students and teachers the ability to work paperless. There is no need to print assignments and hand them out, and there will be no more excuses for lost homework. This also assists with assignments that have been lost or those that were not completed but are still eligible for completion, since all projects are stored with Google Classroom.

The application gives the option for customizing learning for each student. The teacher can assign a lesion to one student, a group of students, or the entire class. And teachers can access the work of each student for the whole of the duration of the course. This option gives the teacher easy access to the progress of the student's work when needed for things like parent conferences, IEP meetings, and answering any question the student might have about their progress.

With Google Classroom, the entire educational process, as it is now known, can be done online. Teachers have a way to post assignments, link videos, suggest resources, and publish their videos to teach their students and help them continue learning. Google Classroom is a one-stop site where students can access their assignments, search for resources, submit their work, and receive feedback along with their grades. The process can also be used for online learning when students are in the traditional classroom by creating a site where actual classroom learning is merged with virtual classroom learning.

Sharing information on Google Classroom makes the process of transferring all information easier. Parents can be invited into the virtual classroom, so they will know what their students are studying and how they are progressing. Topics for discussion can be posted by the teacher so that everyone who has access can share their opinions and thoughts. This sharing process means that any student is free to take part in the classroom, whether they are on a desk in the building or at home in their rooms. Students will often learn more from their peers than they do in a learning environment, and Google Classroom makes this possible.

One of the best features of Google Classroom is the ability of the teacher to create more than one class. Using this feature, a teacher can create a different class section for each additional class they are teaching. This allows the teacher to use the same assignments and resources over multiple platforms or to tailor the information to each class based on the needs of that class.

How Google Classroom Will Enhance Your Teaching

Using Google Classroom can save time for teachers and students and make the entire process of learning much more effective. The application possesses an understandable interface and a level of technology, which makes it easy to use, even while it is well advanced of many other applications. Teachers can concentrate on their work of teaching and not worry about the operation of the online site. There is no need to share or print assignments or schedule time to meet with each student individually. This will help to facilitate the learning process in the future since online learning will significantly decrease the budget needed to operate the school for an entire school year.

While Google Classroom offers many online components that will make life easier for teachers, the benefits for the teacher will significantly improve their ability to teach effectively. One of the best advantages of Google Classroom is that Google will listen to user's comments and consider them when changes to the format need to be made. Here are some of the other ways in which using Google Classroom will improve your teaching methods.

Forms are embedded, so feedback is easily usable and instant. This feature instantly increases student accountability and engagement, not just with their peers but with the classroom material. One way this can be used is to have students complete a quiz while watching a video. The quiz can be graded immediately after watching the video, and any learning gaps can be covered while the material is still available to view again.

Classes must be preplanned, but the process is easy and well worth the effort. One exciting feature of Google Classroom is that teachers can schedule assignments for future completion. A particular task can be scheduled to open on a Monday and close that Friday. This feature gives the teacher some flexibility if they need to be away from the class for any given amount of time. They can use primary assignments from one class to another. This is especially useful for things like grading expectations and the class syllabus.

Collaboration outside of school is even more comfortable. Google Classroom is cloud-based, so it is accessible anywhere and at any time.

Students can work together from home and share information. The teacher can set a video to go live at a specific time, in preparation for a future test.

It is easier to help students who need extra assistance. Google Classroom gives organizational advantages that will make the teacher's life much more comfortable. Classrooms are organized, and the assignments and other information will not get lost. This organization frees up the teacher's time to spend with the students who need more help navigating the class. This assistance will include assisting them with class content, as well as how actually to navigate the Google Classroom site.

Communication is more effective when using Google Classroom. Even more important than being efficient and easy to use, the communication tools on Google Classroom are handy. All of the information is stored on the cloud; nothing can be lost. That means assignments, videos, resources, and communications are always available for teachers and students alike. Absence is no longer an excuse for being behind in work since the communication is seamless. The newly added parent notifications feature will allow parents to remain informed about the activities in the classroom. Once the teacher has added the list of all of the emails of all of the students, the site is ready for all classroom communication. Entering the student into the classroom will automatically give the teacher and the student access to Google Calendar as well as a discussion group and an email group. Adding and removing students is as simple as adding and removing email addresses.

Google Classroom is an easy application to learn. It will take little time and expertise to set up a new classroom. Most new users can set up their classrooms in 1 – 2 hours.

One of the most challenging things for teachers who use online learning platforms is learning how to set them up and use them. Google Classroom is easy to activate and easy to navigate. And Google offers tech support, which includes setting up and integrating the systems for personal use. Once the teacher is familiar with the plan and how it operates, then they can set up the classroom. Google Classroom was explicitly designed to assisting teachers with integrating and understanding the functions of the school and its technology by streamlining online learning and the process of going to virtual learning.

Chapter 2: How to Use Google Classroom

Google Classroom is the platform that ties together all of the Google G Suit Tools for the use of teachers and students. It also acts as an organizer for digital content where teachers can store materials for the class and share them with their students, and everything is done electronically. With Google Classroom, you can choose the features that you want to use, although you will probably like to use every available feature. The flexibility of the product and how easy it is to use, along with the seamless integration of many of Google's most popular tools, have made Google Classroom one of the most widely used of the technical tools in today's world of virtual learning.

Google Classroom is not a stand-alone student information system, course management system, or a learning management system, but there are regularly new functions added to Google Classroom. As the system continues to add more features, Google Classroom will most likely begin to function more like a learning management system. At the moment, it is the best one-stop location for organizing the event of the classroom.

Anyone can use Google Classroom. It is included for anyone to use as a free service with a personal Google account. It is also open for any organization that is already using G Suite for Education or the G Suite for Nonprofits. Using a Google account provided by their school, in most cases, students and teachers can access Google Classroom. And even though the students and teachers will be the primary users of Google Classroom, there are also functions for families, guardians, and administrators.

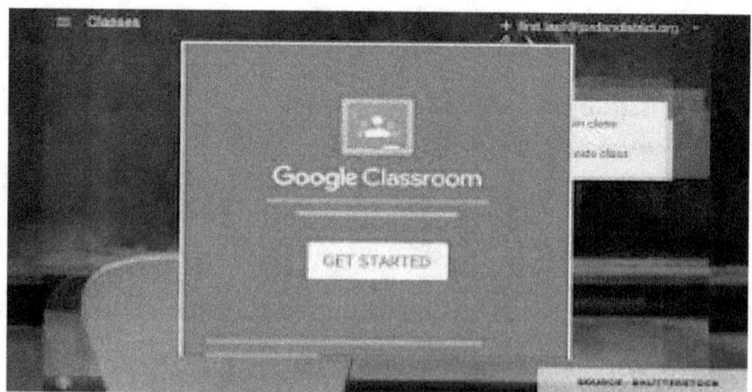

Getting Started on Google Classroom

One of the essential considerations for having Google Classroom is to have Google as a web browser. If you own an Android computer or mobile phone, your device will come with Google as a web browser. Google Chrome is an advanced form of Google web browser, and you can download it to your tablet or mobile phone through the Google Play Store. If you want to use Google Chrome on your computer, you will need to download the installation file while you are in Windows. For the iPhone or iPad, Google Chrome is available for iPhone, iPod Touch, and iPad, and iOS Twelve or later versions. It is available through the App Store on your device.

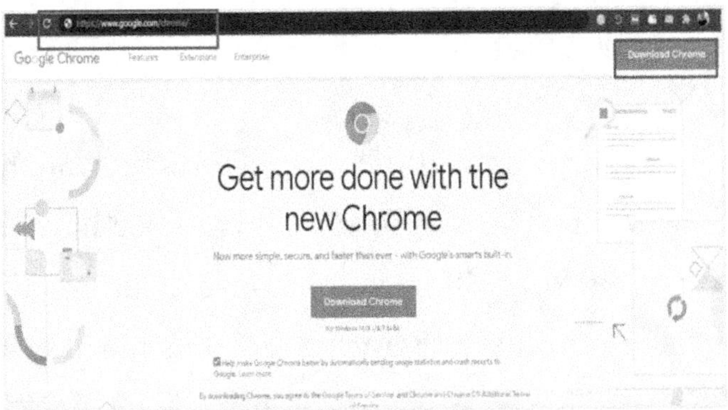

The Main Screen on Google Classroom

The first step in starting your Google Classroom account is to set up your Google Apps for Education account. Google Apps for Education, or G Suite for Education as it is known, is a suite of tools that are based in the cloud for use by public school systems, nonprofit elementary and high school classes, homeschools, and institutes for higher learning. The administration of the school submits the request for this account, and requests are usually approved within fourteen days after submission.

Once your organization is approved, then you will need to create your G Suite for Education account at docs.google.com.

Choose your primary domain, which is the one that was set up by the administration at your institute of learning. You will need to choose a domain that you have administrative access to, which will mean that you have access to change the Domain Name System (DNS) record.

Insert and Manage Student Information and Records

DNS records are created by the DNS server to provide you with important information about the domain or the hostname, particularly the currently used IP address. The IP address is an address that your (or the schools) internet provider assigned to that domain. On your home computer, the IP address is linked to your unique address. You will need access to the DNS if you want to be able to set up your virtual classroom.

The DNS is the key that you need to be able to access the features that will make up your virtual classroom. Here are some of the critical elements that DNS gives you access to:

> ➤ Global server load balancing (GSLB) which allows for fast routing of different

connections between data centers that are
globally distributed

- ➢ Geographical routing to identify the physical location of each of the users on your network to ensure that they are automatically routed to the resources that are closest to them
- ➢ Internet traffic management that reduces the congestion on the network and enables the traffic to flow quickly to the most appropriate resource
- ➢ Cloud migration and data center that will move internet traffic in a controlled manner to the cloud resources from the resources that are on the premises
- ➢ Multi CDN (content delivery network) will route the users of the application to the CDN that will provide them the best experience

As part of the initial sign up, you will be given a fourteen-day free trial with a ten student limit. To bypass this limitation, you will want to verify your domain immediately after registering it. That will ensure two things. The first thing it will ensure is that no one else will be able to use your domain without your permission. The second thing it will provide is that your application will automatically be submitted for the Education upgrade that will give you full access to Google Classroom.

Next, you will decide on the organizational structure that you will be using if the administration at your school has not already set this up. If you are working as part of an established school system, then this step is probably already completed, and it will automatically import when you set up your access to G Suite for Education. You can do it yourself with the option for School Organizational Chart.

Your organizational chart will most likely be set up as a role-oriented structure. In this particular version of the system, the first level of the administrative units is defined by their roles, such as teachers and students. You will need to have this structure in place to be able to describe settings and policies working independently of the school or the school district.

After you have set up the organizational chart, then you will create individual user accounts for anyone who needs to have access to the content you will be posting. This access will include administration, faculty, staff, students, parents, and guardians – anyone who will need to access the content of the Google Classroom. Everyone who needs access will need to have their account and credentials because it is not recommended that users share accounts with other users. Using a CSV upload is by far the best and quickest way to do this.

A CSV upload is an excel file, also known as a Comma Separated Value (CSV) file. It is the fastest method for you to add many users in a short amount of time.

You first need to download the template file from the Google Admin console, using your administrator account. From the **Home** page on the **Admin** console, go the **Users** tab. Download the blank CSV template, which will allow you to open the spreadsheet in the spreadsheet application of your choice. The file will have different columns for adding the various attributes that will appear in the profiles of each user.

Now you will enter the information of the users you want to add. For each user you are adding, you will need to add specific details:

> First name

> Last name

> Email address, using the proper format of username@example.co

> Password – this will need to be at least eight characters

> Organizational Unit Path – you will need to enter a / (forward slash) if there are any users that you want to put into the top level of your organizational hierarchy in the console for Administration; you will only

need to do this if you haven't set up your hierarchy yet

➢ There are other informational columns on the spreadsheet, but they are not mandatory, so do not fill then out if you do not need them. If there is additional information you want to save, then go ahead and enter it now because you will keep this spreadsheet and it will contain all of the user information for the users that you are currently adding. All the information you will need in the future will be saved in one document.

After you finish adding all of the users to the file, then you will need to save it as a CSV file by typing .csv after the name of the file. The maximum size of the CSV file is thirty-five megabytes (MB). One hundred fifty thousand individual records is the maximum number of records that you can add to one file. If the file that you are creating is larger than those parameters, then you will need to separate the information in the file into two or more files before you can save the information and download it. If you need to break up the information, you will need to save each one as a separate CSV file and make sure that you include the column headings over the rows on each spreadsheet file.

After you have saved the spreadsheet and saved it as a CSV file, then you will need to upload it to your computer to add the information to your G suites for Education file information. Go back to the **Home** page on the **Admin** console, again to the **Users** tab, and click the option for **Bulk update users**. Click the option for **Attach CSV file**, and then browse to the appropriate location on your computer and attach the CSV file from where you have saved it on your computer. Click **Upload** and upload your spreadsheet. While the CSV file is downloading, the **Tasks** list will automatically open and show you the progress of the upload of the spreadsheet.

Once you have uploaded the spreadsheet, there might be up to a twenty-four-hour delay before the users can access the information on the Education Suite and appear in the global directory. Once all of the users are added to the system, you will need to supply them with their individual login information, which will be their email address and the unique password that you assigned to them. Supply this information to the user's offline so that they can access their accounts when the data is ready for them.

> ➢ NOTE: You will need to establish a password recovery if you are creating Higher Education accounts for your students. This system will ensure that the users will be able to reset their passwords if they forget their password. For these users, you will set their accounts to the non-admin password recovery option on your **Admin** console. Once you do this, the users can click the option for **Forgot Password** on the page where they sign in, and they will

then receive instructions on recovering or resetting their password. If the user adds an email address or a phone number to their account, the system will use that information to send them their temporary password. If the user has not added this information, then they will be directed to the system administrator for a new password.

➢ To turn on the non-admin password recovery, you will sign in to your **Google Admin** console using your administrator account. Then go to your **Home** page, then to the **Security** tab, and then to **Account recovery**. If all of your users are over the age of eighteen, then you can select all of the users at one time by selecting the top organizational unit. Then choose **User** account recovery, Allow users and non-super admins to recover their account. Then you can instruct the users to set up a recovery email address or a phone number so they will be able to receive recovery instructions for resetting their password if needed.

➤ If you are using your G Suit for Education account for users who are under the age of eighteen, they will not be permitted to add a recovery email address or phone number to their accounts. They do not have the option to reset their password on their own. Any user of any age who is accessing a primary or secondary education account will not be permitted to supply a recovery email address or phone number for a password reset. If they need to reset their password, they will need to contact the system administrator for information.

➤ Set the password requirement that the users must follow to set a password that complies with the requirements you have selected. As the manager of the user's admin, you are responsible for enforcing conditions for the passwords the users set. Help them keep their accounts safe by requiring a strong password with a certain number and specific type of characters. You can see the password the users set, so you can direct users who have weak passwords to select a new one. You can also prevent the users from reusing the password they have already used.

➢ To set the requirements for the user's passwords, sign in to your **Google Admin** console. Then go to the **Home** page, then to **Security** and **Password management**. On the left side of the screen, you will select the organization of users that you are setting the password requirements for. In the **Strength** section, you will set the **Enforce strong password** box. In the **Length** section, you will enter a minimum length and a maximum length for the password requirements. The length can be anywhere between 8 and 100 characters. In the **Expiration** section, you will select the period of time the password will remain valid before it expires. You will also want to click the **Override** selection to keep the setting the same, so if the parent tries to change the settings, they will not be able to.

> ➢ OPTIONAL: If you want users to change their password on the next login, then select **Enforce password policy at the next login**. This policy will force all of the users to change their passwords to meet the requirements you want them to follow. They will never be allowed to reuse old passwords unless you select the **Allow** password reuse setting.

Once you have determined the parameters for the passwords and allowed your users to set their passwords, you will want to monitor their passwords to make sure they have established strong passwords to keep the system safe. Anyone who does not set a strong password runs the risk of someone unauthorized to access their information, and this will put the system and all of the other users at risk of having their data exposed. So sometime after the users have set their passwords, login and check their passwords. You will do this by signing in to your **Google Admin** console, then go to the **Home** page, and then select the **Reports** tab. If you want to see the password strength for each user, then you will go to **Reports > User reports > Accounts**. If you need to look at a graph that contains all of the information about the strength of the passwords, then you will go to **Reports > Apps reports > Accounts**.

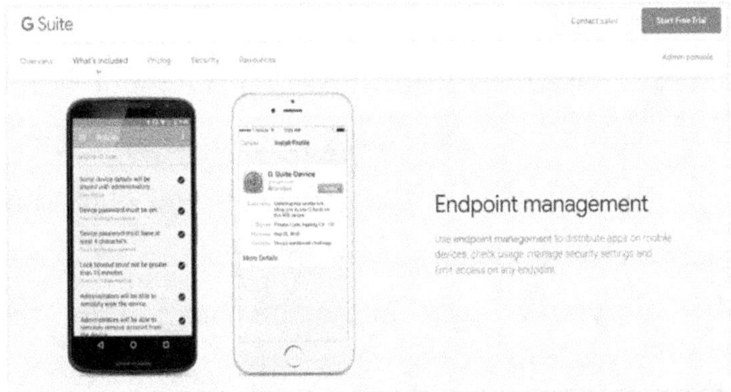

Create and Enter a Class

To begin your first session with Google Classroom, sign in with your Google Apps for Education account, and go to https://classroom.google.com/.

- At the top of the computer page that is marked **Classes**, click the **Add +** to create a class
- Enter the name of the class
- Enter a short description of the class content, the appropriate grade level, or the time for the class in the section that is marked **Section** (this step is optional) and enter all of the details that you want to enter there.
- Select the **Subject** to enter the name of the subject or select a subject name from those that appear in the list when you click that selection (this step is optional)
- If you want to enter the location for the class, then click on **Room** and enter the location you desire (this step is optional)
- Click **Create** to set the class information

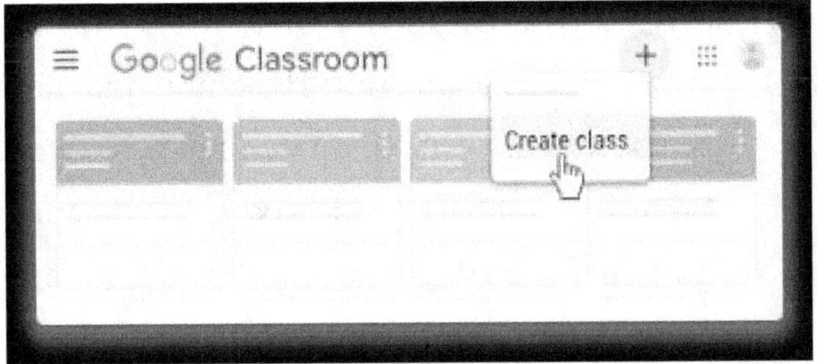

Once you have created the class, Google Classroom will automatically provide a class code that you will provide to the users so that you can invite the students into the class. The class code will also be displayed at the top of the class stream, only on your pages.

There are other options you will be able to use after you have set up your first class in Google Classroom.

> ➤ The administrator of your G Suite for Education may, from time to time, set up a class for you and your students and add all of you to these classes. This is known as a provisioned class. You will then need to

activate the course so that it is visible to your students and any teaching partners that you may want to invite in to assist you. Sign in to https://classroom.google.com/ and on the card for that class, click **Accept**. Now system will ask you to confirm the number of students that you are enrolling in the course and then to select **Accept** again to finalize your acceptance.

➢ You may want to change the theme or image of the class. Login to https://classroom.google.com/ and select the class that you want to change the theme or image of. At the bottoms of the image, click on **Select theme**. Then a gallery of choices will pop up. You can select one of the pictures from the gallery and then click **Select class theme**. You can also click on **Patterns**, and then select a pattern and a color, and then click on **Select class theme**. You can also choose to upload your personal photo to use for the image of the class. To do this, you will open the class and then click on **Upload** photo. Then you can either drag a photo from your collection on your computer to the middle of the screen, or you can select a picture from an internet search on your computer, then choose the image and click **Open**. After you have selected the image you want to use, then click on **Select class theme**.

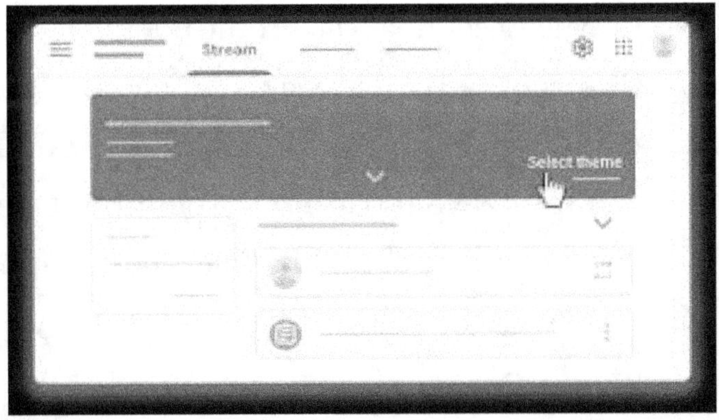

> After you have completed setting up the class, you might want or need to edit the information about the course. Perhaps you have chosen a new name that better fits the content of the study, or the subject matter

has changed. To make this change, you will go to https://classroom.google.com/ and on the class, card click on **More > Edit**. Then enter the new name of other information about the course and then click on **Save**.

➢ When you have set up your Google Classroom account, the information for the Classroom will use the profile photo on your Google Account as the profile photo for your Classroom. If you want to change that photo, you will need to change your profile picture on your **Google Account**. Open your administrator Gmail account, and on the top right of the screen, click on your profile picture. Then click on **Manage your Google Account**. When you have accessed your **Google Account** page, click on **Personal Info**. Under the **Profile** selection, tap your current profile picture. Then you will follow the option prompts on the screen to take a new photo or to choose from your existing images. Then click on

Set Profile Photo. Your profile photo will then change on your **Google Account** and also on your Google Classroom account.

➤ Once you have completely set up a class, you can copy the course. You can copy any archived or active class that you might plan to teach again. When you make a copy of an archived class, then your copy becomes an active class. The only people who can copy a class are the teachers and the co-teachers. The teacher that makes the cop of the course will then become the primary owner of the copy of the class that was made. When you make a copy of a class, the title, section, description of the class, the course subject, all listed topics, the classwork, and the system for grading will all be copied. Any copied questions and assignments will save as draft in the new class. Some of the items will not copy to the new course, and these items include announcements from the teachers, any deleted classwork items, posts from the students, any attachments that you do not have the permission to copy, and any files from Google Sites.

- ➢ At this time, you can only copy a class if you are using the web version of Google Classroom. To copy a course, you will first go to https://classroom.google.com/. When you find the course that you want to copy, then click on **More > Copy**. If there is no option to copy the class, then you are not listed as either the teacher or the co-teacher, and you will not have permission to reproduce it. Once you click on **More > Copy**, if you have permission to copy the class, then a box will pop up where you will be able to edit the title of the course and add any other information you need to designate the class. Then click **Copy,** and the course will be copied. This procedure may take a while, so you are free to leave this page and work on other tasks while Google Classroom is completing a copy of the class. It will notify you with an email when the process is completed.

FAQs for a Copied Class

> For the class **Stream** page, the name, section, and subject will copy, but the room number, class code, and posts and comments will not reproduce.

> For the class **Classwork** page, the listed topics, assignments, quizzes, rubrics that were added to assignments, and class materials and their attachments will copy. Questions will copy as drafts, and attachments will only copy if you have the permission to reproduce them. Google Sites files will not copy, as well as any file that you do not have permission to copy.

> For the **Grades** page in the new copy, this page will remain blank until you add the students in and post their classwork, such as the questions or assignments. Previous classwork posts, like questions and lessons of the initial call, the system you set up for grading criteria, and the categories for grading will all copy to the new class, but the

previous students and their grades will not reproduce.

➢ For the **Peoples** page, the information about the primary teacher will copy, but the information about the students and the co-teachers will not copy.

➢ For the **Settings** page, all of the details about the class, except for the room number, and all of the grading settings, including the grade categories and the calculation settings for the grades, will copy to the new class. The general settings and the class code will not copy to the new class. The general setting will return to their default settings, and a new class code will be generated for the new course.

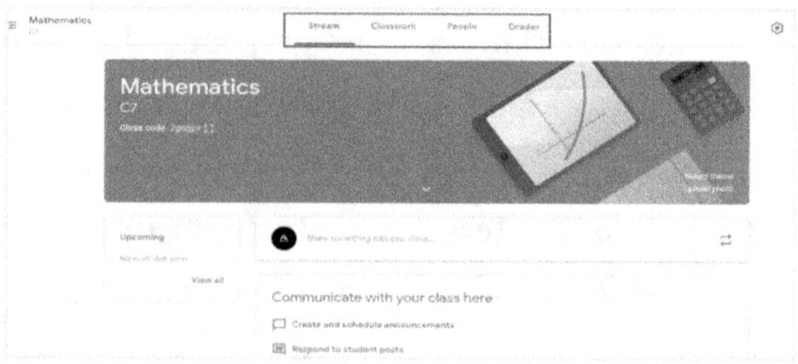

Inviting Your Students to Your Class

When you have set up your Google Classroom account and set up one, or maybe more, classes that you will be teaching, you will need to invite your students into the course so that you can begin teaching them. There are three different methods for inviting your students to enroll in your class.

- ➢ Send a link to the students in their email inviting them to join the class
- ➢ Send an email to invite the students into the class; then they can join the class from that email or in the Classroom itself
- ➢ Share a unique code for the class that the students can then enter in the Classroom to enable them to join the class

If the students encounter any issues with the code or the link, they can request that you reset them, or you can send the students an invitation in their email. There are instructions on the Google Classroom site if any of the students need extra assistance in entering the Classroom. Students can enroll themselves in the class, and if they unenroll themselves, their grades will be automatically removed.

- ➢ To invite students using the invite link, you will first go to https://classroom.google.com/. Each class that you create will have a unique invite link, and you will be able to share the link with your students so they can join your class. On the card for the course, click on **More > Copy** invite link. Then you will send that link to your students by first copying the link and then pasting it into an email to the students. When the students receive your email, they will be able to click on the hyperlink and join your class. If you do not see the option for the **Copy** invite link, you will need to make sure that you have the selection for invite codes enabled.
- ➢ To invite your students using an email invite, you will go to https://classroom.google.com/. You can

send the email invitation to individual students or a group of your students. If you want to invite the students as a group, you will need to use the email alias that is used for the Google Group. You will not need to be either a member or an owner of the group, but you will need to have access to be able to view the members of that group and their email addresses. This function is useful particularly if you want to invite the students of another class to join your course in one of the provisional classes the administrators have arranged for you. To invite students by using an email invitation, click the appropriate class that you want to invite the students into, then click on **People > invite students**. Then you will enter the email addresses of a particular student or a group of students and then click on **Invite**. The students you have invited can then either join the class through the email, or they can go to the card for that class.

➢ To invite students into class using a class code, go to https://classroom.google.com/ and click on **Class > Settings**. Then copy the code listed there so you can paste it into an email, and then send that email to the students that you want to invite into class.

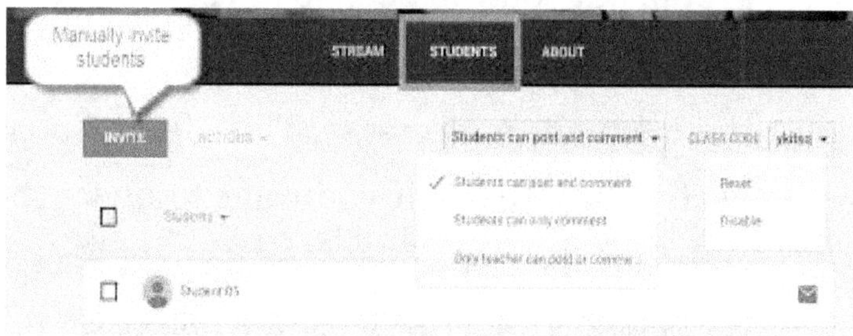

Managing your class code or invite link

For each class you set up, you will have an invite link and a different class code, which is known as the invite code. You share the invite codes with the students you want to invite into the class, so the invite codes are automatically enabled. As the teacher, you can

➢ Reset the invite codes if they are not working correctly.

- Disable the invite codes if you do not want students to join your class after a particular date.
- Enable the invite codes so that new students can join your class. You only need to utilize this function if you have previously disabled the invite codes.

When you select the option to enable invite codes or reset invite codes, Google Classroom will automatically create new invite codes, so the old ones will no longer work.

- Open Google Classroom https://classroom.google.com/.
- Click on the name of the class and go to **Settings**.
- Next to the option for **Manage invite codes**, click the **Down** arrow, and choose one of the available options:
  - Click on **Reset** invite codes to **reset the invite codes**.
  - Click on **Disable** the invite codes to **disable the invite codes**.

- Click on **Enable** invite codes to **enable the invite codes**.
- ➤ Optional operations on this page:
  - If you want to copy the class code, then click on the **Class code** and copy the code.
  - If you want to copy the invite link, then click on the **invite link** and copy the link.

Archive or Delete a Class

When you have finished teaching a particular class, then you can archive it to save the information for later use. When you archive a course, then it will be available to all of the students and teachers in the category for future use. If you do not archive a class when it is complete, then it will continue to show for the teachers and students on their Classes page. Both teachers and co-teachers can archive a class, but only the primary teacher has permission to delete a course. Students do not have permission to either archive or delete a course.

A class that has been archived is put into a separate area to preserve the materials from the course, the work from the students, and any posts that are attached to that class. It will not be seen with your active courses that you are currently teaching on the Classes page. You and your students are allowed to view an archived class for viewing purposes only. If you want to use any of the information from that class, you will need to restore it first. You and your students are still able to access any of the class materials in Google Drive. This availability will include any of the attachments for the assignments and any other work by the students. Students cannot unenroll from a class that has been archived, and this might limit the ability they have to manage the courses they have completed. You can create an unlimited number of classes with your Google Classroom account, but you will want to keep your classroom homepage tidy by only displaying the classes that you are actively teaching. When you have finished teaching a class, you have the option to either archive it or remove it from your Google Classroom page, or you have the option of deleting the course entirely if you are sure that you will never need it again.

How to archive a class

When you choose to archive a class, then it will no longer appear for the students to view. The teacher has the option to view the course and also restore it if that is needed.

> ➢ Open Google Classroom https://classroom.google.com/.
> ➢ Click on the **More** button for the class that you need to archive.
> ➢ In the drop-down menu, click on **Archive**.
> ➢ Click on **Archive** again to confirm your selection. This class will now be removed from your roster of active courses.

How to view a class that has been archived

- ➢ Open Google Classroom https://classroom.google.com/.
- ➢ Click on the **Menu** button.
- ➢ Click on the selection for **Archived Classes**. Any of your archived classes will appear on here. There is a permanent overlay of a theme page that will show it is not an active class. This page is the site where you will restore classes or permanently delete them.

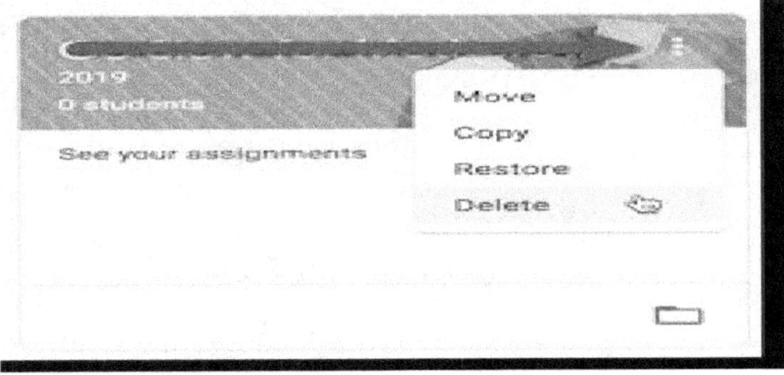

How to delete an archived class

When you want to delete a class entirely, you will need to archive it first. You can't delete a class directly if it is still an active class.

- ➤ Open Google Classroom https://classroom.google.com/.
- ➤ Go to the **Archived Classes** page.
- ➤ Click on the **More** button for that class. From this menu option, you can also restore the course to your active class menu or create a copy of the course.
- ➤ Click on the **Delete** selection. Make sure you select the correct class option because once you delete a class, you can't undo that deletion.
- ➤ Click on the selection for **Delete**.

The class is now permanently deleted from your Google Classroom. However, the course will remain stored in Google Drive. If you have no need to keep or store the files, then you will need to delete them manually from your Google Drive.

Google Classroom Calendar

The calendar you create for the class will remain in your Google Calendar and the calendars of your students. You can remove the calendar from view if you no longer need it, or you can permanently delete the calendar. The calendar for an archived class will stay in the Classroom view until it is deleted. This shows why the calendar for an archived class will still appear in your Google Calendar. You can create a different calendar for different kinds of events.

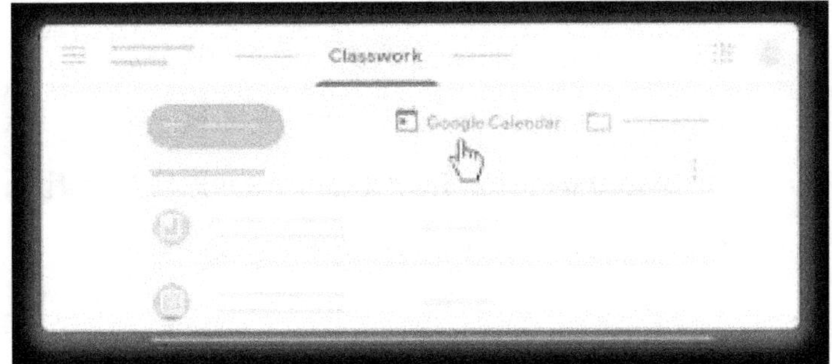

Make a new calendar

You will need to open a browser to create a new calendar since they can't be made from the Google Calendar app. Once you have completed the calendar, then you will be able to locate it in your app as well as in the browser.

> ➢ On the computer, open Google Calendar https://calendar.google.com/.
> ➢ On the computer screen on the left side, next to the option for other calendars, click on the option for **Add other calendars** and then **Create a new calendar**.
> ➢ Add a description and a name for your calendar.
> ➢ Click on **Create** calendar
> ➢ If you need to share your calendar, just click on the calendar and then select the option for **Share with specific people**.

Find a calendar you have created

- ➢ Open Google Calendars
  https://calendar.google.com/.
- ➢ On the computer screen on the left side,
  under the choice of **my calendars**, there
  will be a list of all those calendars that you
  have created.
- ➢ If you want to show or hide the events on
  that calendar, click on the name of the
  calendar.
- ➢ If you need to remove calendar form your
  list of calendars, click on **Options** and then
  Hide from the list next to the name of the
  calendar

Edit the name of the calendar

- ➢ Open Google Calendar
  https://calendar.google.com/.
- ➢ On the computer screen on the left side, find
  your calendar under **my calendars**.

- ➢ Next to the calendar you choose, click on the **Options** and then **Settings and sharing**.
- ➢ In the naming box at the top, type in the new name for the calendar.

Change the color of the calendar

- ➢ Open Google Calendar https://calendar.google.com/.
- ➢ On the computer page on the left side, under the option for **my calendars**, find the calendar you need to change the color of.
- ➢ Next to the calendar, click on the **Options**.
- ➢ Pick the new color for your calendar, or click on the choice to **Add custom color** .

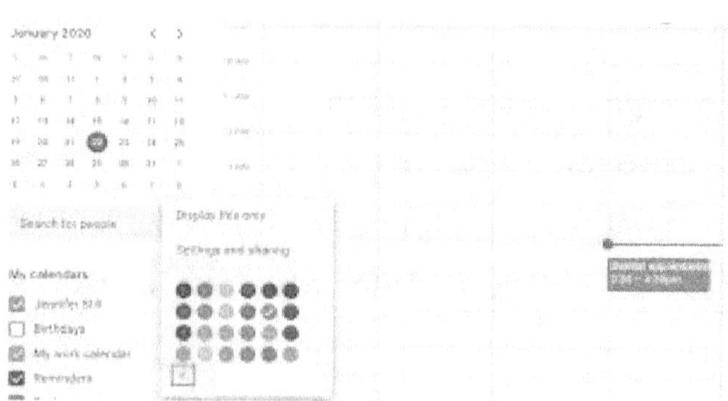

Temporarily hide a calendar

This selection is the best option for those calendars that you only check occasionally.

> ➢ Open https://calendar.google.com/.
> ➢ On the left side, locate the calendar you need to hide. Look under both '**my calendars**' and '**other calendars**.'
> ➢ Click on the calendar and select the option to hide it.

Remove a calendar from the list temporarily

When you do this to remove a calendar from your list of calendars, you will not see the calendar under either 'my calendars' or 'other calendars.'

> ➢ Open Google Calendar https://calendar.google.com/.
> ➢ On the left side, look for the calendar you need to remove. It might be located under

'my calendars' or under 'other calendars.'

> Hover your mouse (let the cursor of the mouse lay over) over the name of the calendar and click the option for **More** .

> Click on the word **Hide** in the drop-down list.

Bring back a calendar when you have removed it

> Open Google Calendar https://calendar.google.com/.

> In the corner on the top right, click on the choice for **Settings** and then **settings**

> In the column listed on the left, locate the calendar that you want to restore.

> Click on Preview

Permanently remove a calendar from your list

When you decide to unsubscribe from a calendar, then you will not be able to see it again unless there is another owner of the calendar who can share the calendar with you again.

> - Open Google Calendar https://calendar.google.com/.
> - In the corner on the top right, click on the option for **Settings** and then **settings**.
> - In the column listed on the left side, choose the calendar that you want to delete permanently.
> - Click on **Remove calendar**.
> - Click on **Unsubscribe**.
> - Click on **Remove calendar**.

Restore a calendar after you unsubscribe from it.

You might accidentally unsubscribe from a calendar that you are still using. Mistakes do happen no matter how careful people are,. Whether or not you will be able to get the calendar back onto your screen after you unsubscribe from it will depend on whether or not the calendar is shared with someone else or owned by someone else. If you owned the calendar, but you did not share it with anyone else (like a co-teacher), then, unfortunately, you will not be able to restore the calendar after you unsubscribe from it. This reason is why removing the calendar from your list is the best option in most instances. If you owned the calendar and you shared it with someone else, and they still have access to it, then you can ask them to find the address of the calendar. You can then use that address to add the calendar back into your Google Classroom account.

Step 1: Instructions for the other person who has access to the calendar

- ➢ Open Google Calendar https://calendar.google.com/.
- ➢ In the corner on the top right, click on the option for **Settings** and then **settings**.
- ➢ In the column on the left, find the shared calendar that you need to restore.
- ➢ Click in the name of the calendar.
- ➢ Scroll on the screen down to the section that is named '**integrate calendar**' and then click on either the **Secret** or the **Public iCal** address.
- ➢ Copy the link that shows there and send that link to you.

Step 2: Follow these steps to restore the calendar to your Google Classroom

- ➢ Open Google Calendar https://calendar.google.com/.

- ➢ In the corner on the top right, click on the option for **Settings** and then **settings**.
- ➢ On the computer screen on the left side, click on **Add calendar** and then **from URL**.
- ➢ Paste the address link of the calendar you are trying to restore from the other person into the URL field.
- ➢ Click on **Add Calendar**. The calendar should now be listed for viewing in your available calendars on the left side of the Google Calendars page.

Delete a calendar

Be very careful before you delete a calendar because there is a good chance you will not be able to restore that calendar. When you delete a calendar, the calendar and all of the attached events are deleted permanently. If you have shared that calendar with other people, they will no longer have access to that calendar and its events. You will never be able to delete your primary calendar, but you will be able to clear off the events listed on the calendar.

> - Open Google Calendar https://calendar.google.com/.
> - In the corner on the top right, click on the option for **Settings** and then **settings**.
> - In the column on the left side, locate the calendar that you need to delete.
> - Click on the name of the calendar.
> - Click on **Remove calendar** and then **Delete** and then **Delete permanently**.

Delete all of the events in your primary calendar

While you are not able to delete the primary calendar, you can delete all of the events on the calendar.

> - Open Google Calendar https://calendar.google.com/.

> On the top of the web page, click on **Settings** and then **settings**.

> Click on the name of your primary calendar, which is located at the top of the list. It will usually be labeled with your first name and last name.

> At the bottom of the page, click on **Delete**. You might need to wait for a few minutes of lag time before you can completely access the features of Google Calendar after clearing off your primary calendar.

Share your calendar with someone else

While you can share your calendar with coworkers, co-teachers, friends, and family, you must use caution when sharing your calendar. Anyone who has full permission with the calendar can share that calendar with other people as well as create and edit events and respond to invitations. There are times when sharing your calendar with others is the best option for you. If you share your calendar with your family, then they will immediately have access to your schedule. You can create a family calendar that more than one person has access to, so they can view the calendar and add events. You can also add a designated person, such as a co-teacher or an administrative assistant, so they can schedule and edit your affairs for you.

Share an existing calendar

> Open Google Calendar https://calendar.google.com/.
> On the computer screen on the left side, find the section marked '**my calendars**.' You may need to click on the selection to expand it for more comfortable viewing.
> Let your mouse hover over the calendar that you want to share, then click the icon for **More** and then **Settings and sharing**.
>> o If you want to share the calendar broadly, so that anyone will have access to it, then you will click on **Access permission** and check the boxes of how you want to share the

calendar by choosing the options in the drop-down menu.

- o If you want to share your calendar with particular individuals only, then you will click on the option for **Share with specific people** and then click on **Add people**. Then add the person or the email address of the Google group you want to share the calendar with. There will be a drop-down menu if you need to adjust their permission settings. Then click on **Send**. Once the recipient has received the email, they will need to click on the link to be able to add your calendar into their list of calendars.

If you are plan to share your calendar with a group, then it is not automatically added to their list of other calendars. Over time the calendar sharing settings will automatically adjust to any changes in the group.

Delegate your calendar

You can assign full permission to other people to manage your calendar for you. It is probably not a good idea for you to give this permission to very many groups or individuals.

> ➢ Open Google Calendar https://calendar.google.com/.
> ➢ On the computer screen on the left side, find the section that is labeled '**my calendars**.' You might need to click on the selection to expand it for more comfortable viewing.
> ➢ Let your mouse hover over the calendar that you need to share.
> ➢ Click on the option for **More** and then **Settings and sharing**.
> ➢ Under the option for **Share with specific people**, click on **Add people.**
> ➢ Enter the email address of your new delegate.
> ➢ Under the selection, **Permission** click on **Make changes and manage to share**.

➤ Click on **Send**.

The delegate you send the calendar to will need to click on the link in their email if they need to add your calendar to their list of calendars. If this person creates an event on your calendar, then the invitations will appear to come directly from you.

Unshare your calendar by removing people from the sharing settings or stop publicly sharing your calendar

- ➤ Open Google Calendar https://calendar.google.com/.
- ➤ On the computer screen on the left side, find the selection for '**my calendars,**' and you might need to click on the choice to expand it for more comfortable viewing.
- ➤ Let your mouse hover over the calendar that you want to unshare. Then click on **More** and then **Settings and sharing**.

- ➢ Under the choice for **Access** permissions, turn off the **Make available to the public**.

  - o To stop sharing your calendar with certain people, choose the option for **Share** with specific people, then next to the person that you want to remove then click on **Remove**

- ➢ If you are sharing multiple calendars, you will need to do this for every calendar that you need to stop sharing.

How to stop sharing your availability information with other apps

If you have made your calendar visible to other people, anyone who tries to contact you when you are not available will receive a notice in one or more of their other G Suite apps. You can remove this notice with a few simple steps.

- ➢ Open Google Calendar https://calendar.google.com/.

- On the computer screen on the left side, find the section that is marked '**my calendars**,' and you might need to click on the choice to expand it for more comfortable viewing.
- Point to the calendar that you need to stop sharing and click on **More** and then **Settings and sharing**.
- Under **access permissions**, you will turn off the **Show calendar info in other Google apps, limited by access permissions.**

Using Google Calendar to Create or Transfer Events

When you create an event with someone else using a Google Meet link, the video conferencing policies that apply to that event are also affected by the scheduling. The availability of particular Google Meet features in a scheduled video meeting will significantly depend on the video conferencing setting that applies to the event organizer of the calendar and the edition of G Suite you are using.

If the organizer for the calendar event has access to particular calling features for video conferencing, like the ability to record meetings, then those will be available for any session that the event planner organizes. If they do not have access to those features, then those features will not be available to them for any meeting that they manage. For this application, the term **calendar event organizer** refers to the person who is the owner of the event on Google Calendar, and this might not be the person who is the actual creator of the event if the event was created on this calendar and transferred to another calendar.

If you transfer an event or create an event on the primary calendar that someone else owns, then the person who is the primary owner of that calendar will be the owner of the event. In these cases, the features that are available for the meeting will be the features that are available under the video conferencing policies that are applied to the other person's calendar. This feature means that if the session is being recorded, then the organizer of the calendar event will receive an email containing the recording. Still, the original event creator does not receive one. If the person you transferred the event to or created the event for cannot record meetings, then you will have no recording of the session. When you create an event on the primary calendar of another person, you will not automatically be invited to the meeting. If you will need to attend the meeting, you will need to add yourself as a guest. If you click on an event on any Google Calendar, it will show who the organizer of the calendar event is.

Creating Assignments

After you complete the process of generating an assignment for your students in Google Classroom, you will have the option to post the assignment immediately, save a draft of the assignment, or schedule the assignment to be posted at a later date. After students have completed their work and submitted it, you can grade the assignments and return them to the students. When you create tasks, you can then post the assignments to one or more classes, post them to individual students, add a category for grading, change the point value, add a date or time for the assignment to be due, add topics and assignments, add a rubric, and turn on the originality reports. You will need to access your Google Account to sign in to Google Classroom when you are doing tasks in Google Classroom.

Create an assignment

> Sign in to Google Classroom https://classroom.google.com/.
> Click on the class on the option **Classwork**
> At the top of the class, click on the option for **Create** and then **Assignment**.
> Enter the name of the assignment and any special instruction you have for it.
> You can continue customizing and editing your assignment. When it is complete, you can post the project, schedule it to be published later, or save it.

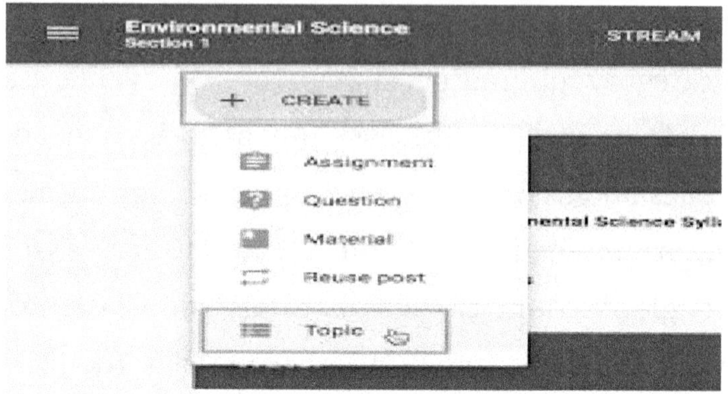

Post the assignment to additional classes

If you post an assignment to students in multiple classes, it will go to all of these students.

> Open Google Classroom https://classroom.google.com/.
> Create the assignment.
> Under the option **For**, click on the **down arrow** and then **select those classes you need to include in the assignment**.

Post the assignment to individual students

Unless you need to post the assignment to multiple classes, you can post the work directly to individual students. You are not able to post to more than one hundred students at one time.

> - Open Google Classroom https://classroom.google.com/.
> - Create the assignment
> - Under **For**, click on the **Down arrow** and then **All students.**
> - Under the selection for **All students,** click on the **Down arrow** , and then **All students option** again to deselect the all students option
> - A list of the student's names will appear under the option for **All students**. Click on the names of the individual students to whom you want to send the assignment.

Add a grading category

You will use this option to add grade categories to organize the assignments. With different grading categories, you will have the opportunity for you and your students to see the category that a task belongs to, like categories for *Essays* or *Homework*. Teachers are also able to view the categories on the **Grades** page.

- ➢ Open Google Classroom https://classroom.google.com/.
- ➢ Create the assignment
- ➢ Under the option for the **Grade** category, click on the **Down arrow** and then **select** the appropriate category from the drop-down menu.

Change the point value

You have the option of changing the assigned point value for an assignment or making the assignment as ungraded. As a default, all projects are given a value of one hundred points.

> Open Google Classroom https://classroom.google.com/.
> Create the assignment.
> Under the option for **Points**, click on the value.
> From the drop-down options, either select ungraded or leave the choice at 100.

Add a date or time for the assignment to be due

The system default gives no due date to any assignment. You can set a due date and/or a time for any assignment to be due.

> Open Google Classroom https://classroom.google.com/.
> Create the assignment.
> Under the option for **Due**, click the Down arrow.

- ➤ Next to the option for **No due date**, click on the down arrow.
- ➤ Select a date on the calendar that opens and click on it.
- ➤ If you want to set a time for the assignment to be due, click on the option for **Time** and then **enter the time** and choose either AM or PM.

With the system defaults, all work is automatically marked wither **Missing** or **Turned in Late** when the due date and time have arrived without the assignment being turned in. If an assignment is scheduled for submission at 9 AM on Tuesday, an assignment that is submitted at 9 AM on Tuesday will be marked as late. Any assignments that are not submitted at that time will be marked as **Missing** until they are submitted, when the designation will be changed to **Turned in Late**.

Add a topic

> ➢ Open Google Classroom
> https://classroom.google.com/.
> ➢ Create the assignment.
> ➢ Under the option for **Topic**, click on the Down arrow.
> ➢ Choose the appropriate option from the two choices.
>> o Click on create topic and add a name to it to make a topic.
>> o Click on a topic from the list that appears to select an appropriate topic.

You can add only one topic to an assignment.

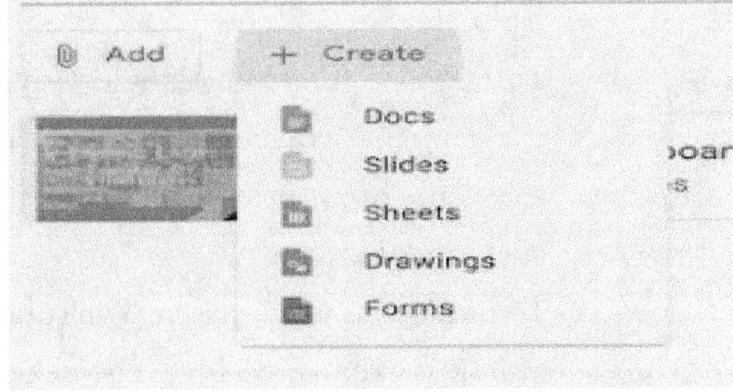

Add attachments

In Google Classroom, you can add on attachments to your assignments. Some of the options are links to articles, YouTube videos, files from Google Drive, or files from your computer.

> - Open Google Classroom https://classroom.google.com/.
> - Create the assignment.
> - Click on **Add** and then choose an appropriate option from the list.
>   - To attach a file from your computer, click on the icon that looks like a paperclip, selects the appropriate file from your computer, and then clicks Upload.
>   - To attach a file from Google Drive, click on the icon for Google Drive, select the appropriate file, and then click on Add.
>   - To attach a video from YouTube, search for the video first. Then click

on the option for YouTube, enter the necessary keywords, and then click on the Search icon. Click on the appropriate video, and then click on Add. If you want to add the video as a link to the video, then just click on YouTube and then URL, enter the information for the URL, and then click on Add.

- To attach a link, click on the link icon, enter the information for the URL, and then click on Add Link.

If you encounter a message that tells you that you do not have the permission to attach a particular file, then click on **Copy**. Google Classroom will make a copy of the file and will automatically link it to the assignment and save the assignment with the attachment in the Google Drive folder for that class. After you add the attachment to the assignment, then you will want to click on the Down arrow that is next to the attachment to choose an option for how the students will interact with the assignment.

> - Students can view files – this option means that all of the students can read the file, but they are not able to edit it.
> - Students can edit files – this option means that all of the students will share the same file to read and make changes to.
> - Make a copy for each student – this option means that the system will create a separate copy for each student so that each student will have their copy of the item from Google Docs, Slides, or Sheets file that has their name on it added with the title of the document. Either the student or the teacher can edit the form. After the student submits the assignment, they will not be able to edit the document until the assignment is returned to them.

The option to choose how the student will interact with the attachment is only available until the assignment is posted. If you find you ever need to remove an attachment, click on the option for **Remove** next to the attachment.

Reuse or create a rubric for an assignment

In Google Classroom, the teacher has the option to reuse rubrics, create rubrics, and grade individual assignments with grading rubrics. A rubric is a small matrix of criteria and their descriptions. The left side of the rubric usually lists the requirements for the expected performance. Across the top of the rubric, you will find the rating scale that gives the students the set of values for grading the quality of their performance for each of the criteria. The criteria tell the students what you are looking for when you grade the assignments and the value of each of the performance levels. You also have the option of exporting rubrics to share them with other teachers. You can provide feedback to the students with unscored or scored rubrics. If you are using a scored rubric, then the scores will be available for the students to see when their assignments are returned to them. There are several parts to a grading rubric:

> Criterion title – this is the name of the criterion that you are evaluating, such as *Homework.*

> Criterion description – this is a short description of the focus of the criterion, such as *The Thesis for your Essay.*

> Level title – this is the title of the specific performance level that the assignment will receive, and these are usually numbers, letters, phrases, or words, such as *Excellent.*

> Level description – under the criterion, this is the description of the characteristics or expectations that need to be met for a specific level of performance, such as a short statement of positive qualities of the assignment.

➢ Total rubric points – this is the total number of points that are available for the grading rubric, such as *100*.

➢ Total criterion points – this is the total number of points that are available for the criterion, such as *30*.

➢ Level points – this is the number of points that are available for a specific level of criterion, such as *10*.

Create a Rubric

You can make up to 50 criteria for each rubric, and up to ten performance levels per standard. Before you create a rubric for an assignment, the assignment will need to have a title.

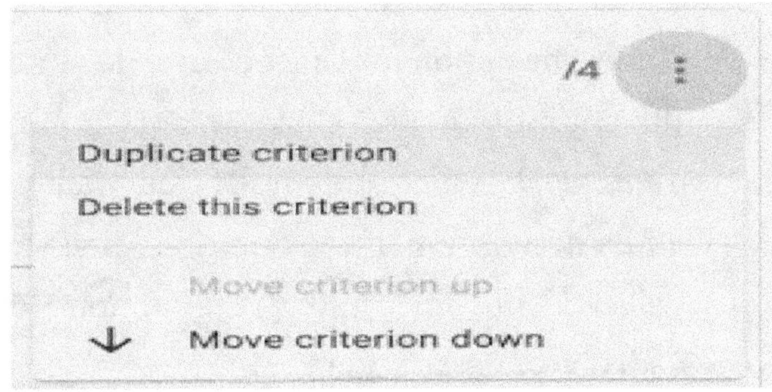

➢ Open Google Classroom https://classroom.google.com/.

➢ Click on the appropriate **class** and then **Classwork**.

➢ Create the assignment with a **title** and then **click on Rubric** and then **Create Rubric**. If you would rather turn off all scoring for the assignment, then next to the option **Use scoring,** click to move the sliding switch to the **Off** position. If you are using a scoring system, then next to **Sort the order of points by**, select the option for **Ascending** or **Descending**. With scoring, you can add the performance levels in any order, and the groups will automatically arrange themselves by point value.

➢ Under the option for **Criterion title**, enter the criterion of your choice, like *Citations*, *Teamwork*, or *Grammar*. If you want to add a description of the criterion, then you will add it now under the option for **Criterion** description.

➢ Under the option for **Points,** you will enter the number of points that will be awarded for each level of performance. The total score of the rubric will update automatically as you enter the point values.

➢ Under the option for **Level title,** you will enter the title for the performance level with a description like *Level A, Full Mastery*, or *Excellent.*

➢ Under the option for **Description,** you will enter the expectations for each level.

If you feel the need to add another level of performance to the criterion, then click on the option for **Add a criterion** and repeat the steps from 8 – 10. If you want to add on another criterion, you can either add on a blank criterion by choosing the option for **Add a criterion** in the lower-left corner or copy a criterion in the criterion click on the criterion box and click the option for **More** and then **Duplicate criterion** and for either option repeat steps 6 – 11. If you want to rearrange the requirements, in the criterion box, click on the option for **More** and then **Move criterion down** or **Move criterion up**. Then click on **Save** to complete the rubric.

Grade categories

Grade categories must add up to 100%

Grade category	Percentage	
Daily Work	50%	×
	Remaining 50%	

Reuse a rubric

You can reuse those rubrics that you created previously. You can view the rubric you want to use first, and then edit that rubric inside of the new assignment is needed. The edits you make in the new assignment will not affect the original rubric. To reuse a rubric, your new assignment will need to have a title.

> ➢ Open Google Classroom https://classroom.google.com/.

- Click on the option for **class** and then **Classwork**.

- Create the new assignment with its **title** and then **click Rubric** and then **Reuse Rubric**.

- Choose the appropriate option – if you want to use a rubric from the same class, then under the option for **Select** rubric, click a title. If you're going to select the rubric from another class, then from the menu for the class, enter the name and click on the title of click on the **Down arrow** and then **select a class** and then **click a title**.

- If you want to view the rubric or edit the rubric, then you can click on **Preview** and then **choose an option**. Then you can edit the rubric by clicking on **Select and Edit** and then **make your changes** and then **click Save**. If you want to

- preview other rubrics that are available for the class, then click on **Back <** or **Next >**.

- Click on the option **Select**.

Add a rubric to an existing assignment

> - Open Google Classroom
>   https://classroom.google.com/.
> - Click on the appropriate class and then
>   **Classwork** and then **the assignment**.
> - At the top of the assignment, click on **More**
>   and then **Edit**.
> - On the right side, click on **Rubric** and
>   choose the appropriate option
>   - Create rubric
>   - Reuse rubric
>   - Import from Sheets

View the rubric for an assignment

> - Open Google Classroom
>   https://classroom.google.com/.
> - Click on the appropriate class and then
>   **Classwork**.
> - Click on the appropriate assignment and
>   then at the bottom, then click on the rubric.
>   If you do not see a rubric, then the teacher
>   has not added one to the assignment yet.

Share a rubric with import and export functions

There will be times that you want to share a Google Classroom rubric with another teacher who is not in your class. You can do this, but you will first need to export the rubric to Google Sheets. Anytime you export a rubric, it will save to the Rubric Exports folder in the folder for the class on Google Drive. After it is saved, you can share the folder or file with a teacher so they can then import your rubric into their classroom assignment. Once they import the rubric, that teacher can edit the rubric into their assignment. Their edits will not affect your original rubric. No one should ever edit the rubric while it is in the Rubric Exports folder. The only rubrics you can import are the ones that are created and exported in Google Classroom. When rubrics are exported, they will save as Google Sheets in the folder for your Rubric Exports. If you try to change this file format or edit the spreadsheets, then the rubrics will not import correctly.

Import a rubric to use it

> Open Google Classroom
> https://classroom.google.com/.
> Click on the appropriate class and then
> **Classwork**.
> Click on **Create** and then **Assignment**
> and then enter the title for your assignment.
> On the right side, click on **Add + Rubric**
> and then **Import from Sheets**.
> Click on the rubric that you want to import,
> then click **Add**.
> Make any needed edits on the rubric now.
> Click on **Save** to save the rubric. If the
> rubric fails to save for you, then have the
> original owner export it again so you can
> import the rubric. Imports can fail if
> someone made or tried to make edits to the
> rubric while it is saved in the Google Sheet
> file folder.

Export a rubric to save it for others to use

➢ Open Google Classroom
https://classroom.google.com/.

➢ Click on the appropriate class, then click on
Classwork and then the assignment.

➢ At the bottom of the assignment, click on
the rubric.

➢ At the top of the rubric, click on **More** and
then **Export to Sheets**.

➢ Click on close to return to your **Classwork**
page.

➢ When you are back on the page for the
Classwork, on the top of the page, click on
the **Class Drive** folder and then
Classroom.

➢ Choose the appropriate option

    o To share just one Rubric, open the
folder for the **Rubric Exports** and
then right-click the rubric you need
to export.

- If you intend to share the entire folder, then right-click on the folder marked **Rubric Exports**.
- ➢ Select the option for **Share** and then enter the name or the email address of the teacher you want to share with.
- ➢ Click on **Send**.

Edit the rubric for an assignment

If there are changes you need to a rubric or delete the rubric entirely, you will need to do this before you begin grading the assignment. Any changes you make to the rubric will only affect the assignment that you are in currently.

- ➢ Open Google Classroom https://classroom.google.com/.
- ➢ Click on the appropriate class and then **Classwork**.
- ➢ Click on the assignment, and then at the bottom of the assignment, click on the rubric.

- In the corner on the top right of the assignment, click on **More** and then on **Edit**. This option will only be available until you begin grading the assignment with the rubric.
- Make any changes that are needed and then click on **Save**.

Delete the rubric for an assignment

This option is not available after you begin grading the assignment with the rubric.

- Open Google Classroom https://classroom.google.com/.
- Click on the appropriate class name and then click on **Classwork**.
- Click on the assignment you want to delete the rubric from. At the bottom of the assignment's page, click on the rubric.
- In the top-right of the page, click on **More** and then click on **Delete**.
- To confirm the deletion, click on **Delete**.

Grading Assignments

For the grading system that you use, you have the option to choose Weighted by Category or Total Points. In either system, the grades will be calculated for you, and then you can let the students check their overall grades listed for the class. If you do not want to use a grading system, then you can choose to assign no overall grade. If you select this option, the grades will not be calculated for the assignments, and the students in the class will not be able to check their overall grades. You can also assign grading categories for specific categories. If you choose to set a grading system, then the grades will be calculated continually during the class. If you begin the same class but with a new semester or term and you want to start a new course of grades, you will need to create a new class.

If you are using the Total Points Grading system, then an overall grade will be calculated for you by dividing the total number of points that a student earns by the total points of points that are possible to achieve in the class. You can set the point values and create grade categories for the classwork in every category. If you are grading with the weighted by category grading system, then you will assign weights by percentages to grade the categories. Then an overall grade will be calculated for you. After you select the grading system, then you can add categories for the grades. If you are using the system for Weighted by Category grading, then you are required to use grading categories. They are not mandatory with the Total points grading system or the No overall grade system. If you are exporting grades to the Student Information System (SIS), then the Classroom grade categories will not transfer to the system.

Select a grading system

You will need to be in the web version of Google Classroom to select a system for grading. It will not work in the mobile app.

- Open Google Classroom https://classroom.google.com/.
- Click on the appropriate class name and then click on **Settings**.
- Go to the **Overall grade calculation** and then select the appropriate option
  - No overall grade – grades will not be calculated for the student's assignments, and students will not see an overall grade for the class.
  - Total points – this will divide the total point that the student earns by the total points that are possible for the class. Students will be able to see an overall grade.
  - Weighted by category – this will add the scores across the categories, and this option will let the students see an overall grade.
- If you want to make the overall grades visible to all of the students on their profile page, then click on the **Show** option. This

option will not be available if the **No overall grade** option is chosen.

> ➢ In the top-right corner of the screen, click on **Save**.

Create grading categories for Total points grading or No overall grade

For these grading options, you can assign default point values to the grading categories that you create. You will need to be in the web browser version of Google Classroom, as this function will not work in the app.

> ➢ Open Google Classroom https://classroom.google.com/.
> ➢ Select the name of the appropriate class and then click on **Settings**.
> ➢ Next to the selection for **Overall grade calculation**, select the option for **Total points** or **No overall grade** from the drop-down menu.

➢ Under the **Grade,** categories click on the option for **Add Grade Category**.

➢ Choose the appropriate grade category.

➢ Under the selection for Default points, enter any whole number of your choice.

➢ If you need to add another grading category, do that now.

➢ In the top right-hand corner of the page, click on the option for **Save**.

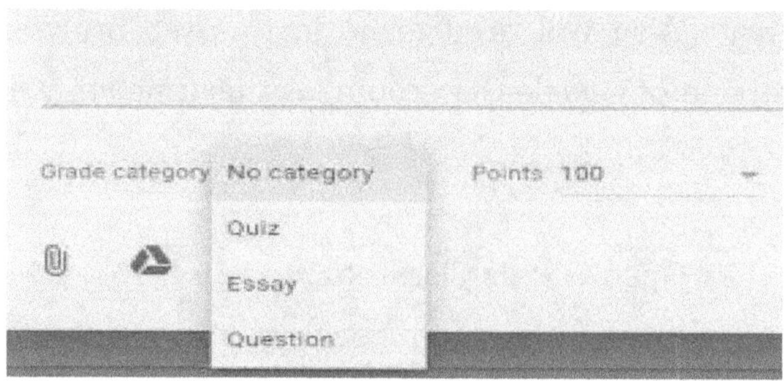

Create grading categories for grading with Weighted by Category

If you are using this option for grading, then you will need to assign percentages to the categories you create for grading purposes. You will need to be in the web browser version of Google Classroom, as this function will not work in the app.

> Open Google Classroom https://classroom.google.com/.
> Select the name of the appropriate class and then click on **Settings**.
> Besides the selection for **Overall grade calculation**, click on the **Weighted by category** selection from the drop-down menu.
> Under the selection for **Grade** categories, click on **Add Grade Category**.
> Enter a category for grading.
> Under the selection for **Percentage**, enter any whole number.
> If you need to add another grading category, then you will do it now.
> In the top right-hand corner of the screen, click on **Save**. Your categories will need to

add up to one hundred percent, or the changes will not save.

Remove a grading category

You have the option of removing the grading categories. If you remove them, it will remove the grading category from the classwork it corresponds to, but it will not delete the classwork itself.

- ➢ Open Google Classroom https://classroom.google.com/.
- ➢ Click the cursor on the name of the appropriate class and then click on **Settings**.
- ➢ Next to the grading category that you need to remove, then click on **Remove**.
- ➢ For the weighted by category grading system, you will either need to adjust the remaining categories or add a new category to make the totals add up to one hundred percent.
- ➢ At the top of the screen, click on **Save**.

Managing the Grade book

On the page for Grades, you can view and then update your grade book. You can view the student submissions, enter their grades, and return graded work to them. The students will receive their grades when you return the work to them. Only the teacher can view the Grades page.

Open your grade book

There are two places where you can open your grade book.

> ➢ Open Google Classroom https://classroom.google.com/.
> ➢ Select the appropriate option
>> o On a selected card for a class, click on Open grade book.
>> o In a particular class, at the top of the page, click on Grades.

View submissions from students

On the page for Grades, you can view the submissions, grade them, and then return the submissions to the students. The grade status or the work will be color-coded -- the color red for missing work, the color green for work that has been turned in or the draft of a grade, and black for work that has been returned. Anything else that is colored is based on the theme of the class and does not indicate grade status or work status.

- ➤ Open Google Classroom https://classroom.google.com/.
- ➤ Click on the appropriate class and then select **Grades**.
- ➤ Point at any cell that corresponds with a student's assignment, then click on **More** and then click on **View submissions**.
- ➤ When you are viewing the submissions from a student in the grading tool, you can enter the grade. Any grades that are entered here will automatically sync to the **Grades** page.

View assignments

Before you view the student's assignment, you can view the status of the work the student is doing and the number of students you have in each category.

> ➤ Open Google Classroom https://classroom.google.com/.
> ➤ Click on the appropriate class.
> ➤ At the top of the computer page for the class, click on the selection for **Classwork**, and then the assignment, and then click on **View assignment**.
> ➤ On the page, for **Student work,** you will see the names of the students and the number of the students in the class grouped by their work status
>   - ○ **Assigned** – this is work that the students still need to turn in, and this will include any work that has not yet been submitted or is missing.
>   - ○ **Turned in** – this is student work that the students have turned in.

- o **Graded** – this is the work that you have graded and returned to the students.
- o **Returned** – this is ungraded work that you have returned to the students.
- o To see all of the students in a particular category, click on the category.
- o To see the submissions from a particular student, on the left side of the screen, click on the student's name.

Enter grades and return work

You can return submissions to the students after they have been graded, or return them without assigning a grade. Any grade that you enter will save as a draft until you click on Return to set the grade. When you return the submissions to the students, they will receive a text or an email notification, so they will know when their

assignments have been returned and are ready to
view.

> Open Google Classroom
  https://classroom.google.com/.
> Click on the appropriate class and then
  select the option for **Grades**.
> If you are going to enter a grade for the
  assignments, you will do it here.
> If you need to return the assignment to the
  students, then click on **More** and the
  Return and confirm.

Enter grades on the student work page

> Open Google Classroom
  https://classroom.google.com/.
> Click on the appropriate class.
> At the top of the computer page, click on
  Classwork, and then click on the
  assignment, and then click on **View
  assignment**.

- If you need to open and review any files that the student has attached, click on the thumbnail and view it.

- The system will always default to 100 for a point value. If you need to change this, then click on the point value, and then enter a new value or select the option for **Ungraded** and then click on **Update**. If you are using decimal grades, the system will support two digits after the decimal point. If you use more than two digits, the system will round the numbers up to the next two-digit option.

- Enter the grade in the space that is next to the name of the student. The rate will save automatically.

- Enter the grades for any other students that need grading.

When you return the assignments to the students, they will then receive their grades.

Enter the grades in the grading tool

You can enter the grades and give personalized feedback to your students using the Google Classroom grading tool. A level of 100 is the default denominator for grading, but you have the option of changing that to any whole number that is greater than zero. You can adjust the grade denominator any time you want to. Any changes that you make to the grade denominator will only affect the assignments that have not been returned to the students. Any work that has been returned will maintain its original grading denominator.

> - In the grading tool, open the assignment from the student.
> - Click on the option for **Grading**.
> - Under the selection for **Grade**, enter the grade assigned to the assignment.

Returning Work to the Student or Downloading their Grades

Students can't edit any of the files that are attached to the assignments until you return the assignments to them. When you have returned the work to the students, they will receive a text or email notification if they have signed up to receive these. You can return assignments and other classwork to more than one student at a time and with or without a grade.

Return an assignment to the student from the work page

> Open Google Classroom https://classroom.google.com/.
> Click on the appropriate class.
> At the top of the computer page, click on **Classwork**, and then click on the assignment, and then click on **View assignment**.
> In the space besides the name of every student who has an assignment that you

need to return, click on the box to select it and then click on **Return**, and then confirm. If you want to use the option for **Return**, you will need to choose the name of at least one student.

Return an assignment to the student from the grading tool

When you return the assignments to the students, they will be able to view their grades. The grades and the feedback will be automatically synced to Google Classroom by the grading tool.

- Open Google Classroom https://classroom.google.com/.
- Click on the appropriate class.
- At the top of the computer page, click on **Classwork**, and then click on the assignment, and then click on **view assignment**.
- Open the assignment from the student.
- Enter the feedback or the grade.
- If you need to return the work to the student, then click on the option for

Return in the corner on the top right of the page.

➤ If you need to return assignments to more than one student

- o Click on the selection marked **Down** arrow next to the option for **Return**, and then click on **Return multiple submissions**.

- o Besides the names of the students, you need to return assignments to, check the box, and then click on **Return**.

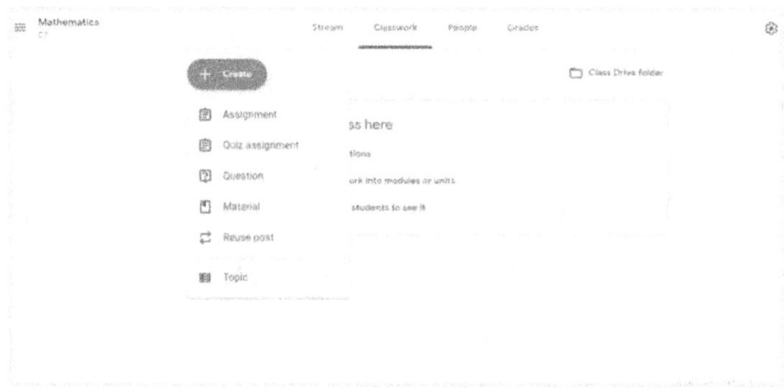

Apps That Work With Google Classroom

For teachers engaged in virtual learning, Google Classroom is the one tool they must have to ensure a successful classroom experience. Teaching students virtually is infinitely more complicated than teaching a classroom full of people, and keeping them engaged and involved is one of the most challenging aspects. Sometimes you might find it necessary, or even merely helpful, to integrate an app from another site into your lesson to make the course more stimulating and exciting. These websites and apps will make your Google Classroom experience even better, and all of them will integrate seamlessly into your Google Classroom classes. Most of them are entirely free; although some of them do offer paid options that include upgrades, the free versions of the apps provide plenty of features worth exploring that are free.

Curiosity.com offers exciting things to read on almost any subject you can imagine. The short articles are easily assigned to your Google Classroom class with one easy mouse click. Ads support the site and the content is better suited to students in high school or middle school.

Edpuzzle will allow you to upload your video and turn it into an interactive lesson. You have the option to add notes, audio, or questions so that students can view the content and then learn the material at their own pace. You can monitor their comprehension and progress with the tracking feature, and this site will easily integrate with Google Classroom. The plan lets you store up to twenty videos at one time.

Flipgrid is a site that allows you to assign topics to the students that they will respond to by recording short videos. This option is an excellent alternative to whole-class calls like Zoom meetings because it gives students who usually would not participate in the discussion the opportunity to be heard. The assignments and grids easily share with Google Classroom.

Google Cast for Education is a simple extension in Google Chrome that makes it easy for you to share your computer screen with anyone. In the virtual classroom setting, the students can share their screens with the teacher, and then the teacher can share those screens with the remainder of the class through Google Classroom.

Listenwise posts new current events podcasts daily that are free to use and share with your students in Google Classroom. The audio lessons are short, so they are the perfect option to begin a discussion on current events or to use for morning meetings. The Premium option offers access to an extensive library of podcasts with interactive transcripts, quizzes, and lessons for a nominal fee, with a ninety-day free trial.

Nearpod is a collaboration tool that is easy to use and has many applications for online education processes. The teacher will begin a board by posting a comment or a question, and then the students will add their thoughts and answers. There is also an option to share pictures. This site is a great way to review for tests or introduce prompts for writing, and it will integrate seamlessly into Google Classroom.

Quizizz helps your students review the information they are learning in the classroom. You can create your quiz or use one of the thousands that are already created on the site. You can assign quiz games for homework or host them to live during a class session. Each assignment can be customized to allow for a certain number of attempts at the answer and to show students the correct answer.

Science Buddies needs to be the best friend for every science teacher. The site is full of experiments, lesson plans, and videos, and everything on the site is searchable by subject and grade level. This site is also a must-see for science fairs since it offers an enormous group of project ideas, planning tools for science fairs, and loads of resources for scientific methods. When you pair this site with Google Classroom, you will gain access to extra assessments and quizzes.

Workbench has an extensive collection of shareable videos and lessons on almost any subject. You can create your classes or use one of theirs. You can add in a video, give detailed instructions, and set out guidelines for entire projects for the students to prepare using the resources on this site.

CK-12 offers various resources for every grade and every subject, and the topics are all covered in texts, lessons, exercises, and videos. You can assign any of these items in your Google Classroom, and the subject completion and the subsequent grade will automatically be recorded in the online Gradebook for the class.

DOGONews offers news articles that are easy for kids to read and enjoy so that they will be more interested in information and discussions around current events. All items can be assigned for reading, and they are marked with guidelines for interest and reading level and suggestions for lesson plans.

Explain Everything is an app with a built-in whiteboard, and you will use it just like any other whiteboard in your classes. It will also allow you to record your interactions with your class and share them through Google Classroom for the students to view later.

GeoGebra does not look fancy at first glance, but it has plenty of functions that will bring the concepts of math alive for your students. The site has hundreds of resources that anyone teaching math will love to use, and that includes using the online graphing calculator. The subjects included cover everything from high-level calculus down to basic math. The site makes it easy to share quizzes, exercises, and lessons with the students.

Mathgames is the perfect online site for any teacher who teaches math to elementary school students. The site offers free practice games to go with the lessons.

Chapter 3: Benefits of Using Google Classroom

Google is easily recognizable anywhere you go, and it is hard to avoid seeing depictions of some of the most popular tools on Google, like Gmail, Google Docs, and Google Calendar. These are now known as the best way to get your work done and remain organized while you do it. These tools are easy to use, collaboration friendly, and they have completely changed how people store information online as well as how they work together and communicate with each other. Google Classroom is an entirely user-friendly platform that brings the benefits of digital collaboration and paperless sharing to the online classroom, making it easier for students and teachers to connect in the classroom. This platform is used by millions of students and teachers to conduct virtual learning all over the world, making it easy to see why Google Classroom is the preferred choice of so many.

While Google Classroom is not technically an LMS (stand-alone learning management system), new functions are regularly added to make using Google Classroom more in-depth and more user-friendly. This tool is the one-stop shopping experience for organizing and conducting your online virtual learning classroom. Since Google Classroom is a free service that is available to anyone with an active personal Google account, then Google Classroom is there for use by anyone and everyone. Organizations that use G Suite for Nonprofits or G Suite for Education can also take advantage of the features of Google Classroom. The teachers and students will have access to the characteristics of Google Classroom by using the Google account that is provided by their school.

Benefits and Advantages of Using Google Classroom

Education for Everyone – Not only can you set up Google Classroom for teaching students online, but teachers can set up Google Classroom arrangements for themselves and their colleagues so they can use the features to conduct sharing of information and faculty meetings as well as classes for professional development.

Completely paperless – While it might be difficult to imagine conducting classwork without using paper, Google Classroom makes an entirely paperless experience a reality. You can hand out assignments and study materials, receive assignments back for grading, and share information with your students entirely online. This experience eliminates the need for printing copious amounts of paperwork and worrying that they will get lost. And the work will never be lost since all Google apps are cloud-based so that the work will save automatically. Students have the freedom to complete assignments wherever they happen to be located, and teachers have that same freedom.

Streamlined assignment process – With the click of a button, you can create an assignment and distribute that assignment to the entire classroom. The student can return the work to the teacher in the same quick and easy way. You can do all of these functions and more with the features of Google Classroom. Once you have created and distributed an assignment, you will be able to see at a glance who is still working on the assignment and who has already submitted it. You will be able to add feedback to the returned assignments to guide the success of your students. The teacher can also track the history of an assignment so that you can see how productive a particular student is during class time. And Google Classroom will automatically time-stamp all work that is submitted, so there will never be any confusion about whether the work was turned in on time or not.

Document availability – One of the best features of Google Classroom is the ability to utilize the features of Google Docs. This area is the place in the cloud where Google stores all of the documents that teachers generate. They can be stored online and then shared with an infinite number of people whenever needed. Your assignments, calendars, announcements, class notes – any document that you create for your class will be waiting for you safely stored in the cloud. Google Docs will keep all of your documents in personalized and organized file folders. Any document that you share will be available to the recipients immediately. This storage ability eliminates the need to continuously send emails to share information with students and fellow teachers.

Availability of apps and add-ons – Google Classroom is available as a mobile app on both android and iPhones, so anyone with a mobile phone can access Google Classroom will full functionality. When announcements and assignments are posted in the classroom, the students will receive a notification on their phone. Teachers can also post announcements and assignments from their phones. And many learning apps can be used with Google Classroom, making the classroom experience diverse and exciting.

Single student information – Using this feature, the teacher can view all of the work for one student for the entire class year. All of the work the student has submitted is available on one screen for easy viewing. This feature makes IEP meetings and parent conferences much more comfortable to conduct. Any work that the student is missing will show here also. And the Guardian Summaries feature allows the families of the students' easy access to view their progress.

Tips and Guidelines for Using Google Classroom

The longer that a product is available for use and the more often that people use it, the more likely it is that people will develop guidelines and tips to make using the product more accessible. This assessment is accurate with Google Classroom.

If you don't get to posted and packaged assignments during class time, try to hide and save them, but don't delete them. Teachers are not allowed to hide assignments that have already been posted in Google Classroom. Think of all of those times that you created a fantastic lesson, complete with video clips and discussion questions, and a short quiz at the end to test the student's knowledge. Now imagine that the class session slips by faster than you thought it would, and you didn't get to the fantastic presentation you had prepared. What do you do? You can post it in the classroom and hope no one starts it, or you can completely discard all of that beautiful work. With Google Classroom, you have a third option: you can save the assignment in a dummy classroom that only you can access. Call this classroom Storage or Staging or anything you want to name it. You will not attach student's names to this classroom. You will take the new assignment to the dummy classroom and post it there until you are ready to use it and delete it from the regular classroom for the moment.

Before you begin a presentation, assist your students by adding evaluation ability into all of your private comments. You will do this by copying and pasting the template into the document before sharing it with the class. You can include emojis for quick feedback, criteria for success, and overall evaluation in your comments. By putting all of this information into the document before submitting it to the students, you can give the students feedback that is informative and accurate while the presentation is going on.

With Google Classroom, you can get an immediate idea of the progress of your students as well as letting them know what they are learning and why. It is easy to post self-assessments in classrooms in Google Classroom, especially in those units for teaching math subjects. These assessments are a powerful but simple method for knowing where the students judge their progress. This will help you plan future lessons and see if the material needs to be covered again. And when you are posting assignments, you can include a short section called 'learning target' which answers the age-old question all students ask eventually –'why are we doing this?'

There are occasions when you will need to share class information with other teachers. If you are teaching specialty classes, then you might need to post the same information to multiple classrooms, something you can easily do when you are using Google Classroom. You might also need to share your classroom information with other teachers who also teach the same students so that they can plan their classroom times and activities. And you can see what other teachers are doing in the same classes you are teaching, in case they have an excellent idea. If you are sharing classroom information with other teachers, make sure you turn off the notifications from those classrooms, so your email will not be overloaded with messages that mean nothing to you.

Try to set aside weekly times for the students in your homeroom to have time to review their email inboxes and organize their classroom assignments. Young people like to text with each other, and most of them find email to be boring. But in Google Classroom, the dialogue that is sent through the emails is invaluable for the student's progress. You can monitor their individual progress by posting assessments for the students to complete. You can post announcements about future events and email particular students to remind them to submit a missing assignment. You can even make private comments in the classroom to post feedback to a student that they will receive in the form of an email. The students must check their email at least once each week to get the information that is stored there. You have the option of setting aside class time once each week to give the students time to clear out their emails.

One simple and easy way to keep your assignments organized is to number them. It will help you keep your files contained in the classroom as well as in Google Drive. Then when you need to find an assignment quickly, you use the keyboard search shortcut of **Control + F** by holding the Control key down while you press the F key. This function will bring a popup box onto the screen, and then you type in the number you are searching for, and the results will be highlighted on the screen. If you are using a Mac computer, the search function is **Command + F**. This can also help the students to find assignments quickly.

Google Docs can help you create a syllabus for the class that is a live document that can be used all year and edited as needed. You will be able to highlight important dates, schedule any daily assignments, and add links to complementary outside sources. You can even make the student's day better by adding links to the appropriate assignment on the syllabus. This ability will also help you break down your tasks into smaller parts if needed. Working on learning projects is essential for overall comprehension and growth, and it is best if longer projects are completed in short segments to facilitate learning and understanding. This division of knowledge can also help guide those students who are not comfortable with managing large projects. You can build due dates for each segment of the project directly into the syllabus.

Make your assignments a package deal by including all the information in one place. You will need to address fewer questions from the students if you include as much information as possible when you post the assignment. It will also give your students more infrequent occasions for making excuses when completing the projects. Start by giving each task its own dedicated number to make it easy to locate in the classroom. Include detailed instructions for the expectations of the assignments, as well as learning goals that are easy for the students to understand. Explain your grading system and requirements and how the work will be graded, as well as the weight it carries in their overall grade. Let the students know if there will be any class time devoted to working on the assignment. Give specific instructions for how to turn in the job, and include all links and attachments in the original assignment post.

Motivating Your Students on Google Classroom

Every teacher knows it can be difficult enough to motivate some students while they are sitting in the same classroom with you. It becomes even more challenging to encourage them when they are miles away and only available by computer or mobile phone. When you are dealing with students, it is imperative to know what motivates them to get the best possible performance from them. Most students are encouraged by four key things, and those are relevance, relatedness, competence, and autonomy.

Relevance is vital for most people, but more, especially for students. They cannot yet view the big picture of life and see how every event is built on the events that came before it. They want to know how this task fits into their lives and why they should care about it. There will be students who just do their work and don't complain or cause problems, but you will always have those who want to know the 'why' behind everything. If possible, create opportunities for the students to become involved in what they are learning. If you are teaching American history, you might take a virtual tour of an actual army establishment that was in use during Revolutionary War. For a science class, you can go inside a hurricane or a tsunami, or see how candy or trash bags are made. Since you are already doing virtual learning, it makes sense to take advantage of virtual learning apps and sites. Google Classroom will allow you to access many different learning sites for videos and demonstrations.

Relatedness means the students want to connect with you as a person and not just as their teacher or guide, and creating positive relationships with your students will go a long way toward keeping the classroom environment healthy. This relatedness is even more critical in the virtual classroom because the students do not need to make a connection with you if they do not want to. As a teacher, you will need to do everything in your power to make a connection with your virtual students. Much of this will depend on your teaching style because not everyone is comfortable with speaking to their students on a personal level. You might begin by reaching out to each student once a week to get their feedback on the activities of the prior week to see if they need any extra assistance. This communication will allow you to connect with the student individually and still keep the conversations based on schoolwork. Email in Google Classroom is a great way to keep the lines of communication open.

Students will often worry about their level of competence in a particular subject. Everyone has their favorite topics, and people tend to do a better job in the topics they like to study and learn about. Your students will be able to complete the assignments better if they feel they have the ability to complete the work. Many people will not even begin a task if they do not think they possess the skills needed to complete it correctly. Make sure your instructions are brief and precise, and any links that are attached to the assignment are easy to reach. Adding the weekly self-assessments in Google Classroom will also allow the students to let you know where they feel their level of competence falls.

When it comes to autonomy, students are king! They like to have choices for completing their assignments, and the more options they have, the more in control they feel they are. Some teachers want to assign all of the jobs at the beginning of a specified period, such as a week or a month, and then allowing the students to complete the assignments at any time in that time period. Some teachers like to make choice boards that will enable the students to pick lessons from different activities, as long as the a1ssignments are completed correctly in the right time period. Still, other teachers like to assign a particular outside website for the students to visit on a predetermined basis so that the teacher can monitor their progress. With Google Classroom, it is easy to suggest outside websites for your students to access that you will be able to observe.

It is also essential to keep the parents and guardians involved in their student's work, and this is easy to do with Google Classroom. Parents and guardians can communicate with their child's teachers through Google Classroom, and the teachers can send regular emails to the parents and guardians to keep them informed of the student's progress. You can also regularly gather reports about and examples of the student's classwork to use when conducting progress reports with the parents and guardians of the students.

When used correctly, Google Classroom will help you streamline the processes needed for managing classwork. You will save hours of work giving feedback, grading and returning assignments, collecting assignments, sharing announcements and class information, and scheduling assignments, all by utilizing the built-in features of Google Classroom. The available strategies and reliable workflows of the site will make your work as a teacher more efficient.

Chapter 4: Comparisons for Google Classroom

The industry for online learning is rapidly growing. Many online learning services are available for classroom learning, and each one has its advantages and disadvantages. Knowing all of these features can be a daunting task. Google Classroom is an online course platform that offers a safe environment for learning where students will be able to learn with online courses. The world's three technology companies for consumer use that are the most prominent all have a Classroom tool for teachers and students to use. This means that Google, Microsoft, and Apple are all in direct competition with each other for a share of the online virtual learning market. All three offer unique features that are usually found only in learning management systems, although none are technically learning management systems. It is essential to know what all three offers when deciding to choose one for virtual learning.

Comparing Google Classroom to Apple and Microsoft

Google Classroom – This service is offered free with Google's G Suite for Education. It is compatible with Android devices as well as iOS devices and any web browser. It is estimated that, globally, Google Classroom has more than twenty million students and teachers using the service. For standard features, it offers teachers the ability to share and create assignments, feedback on student work is easy and streamlined, the students can collaborate online, and there is an option for the guardians of the students to receive updated progress reports.

Google Classroom was the first of the big three online classrooms, launching in 2014. Google has continued to make a steady stream of new features available for its platform, and many of those were designed using feedback from real users of the product. Google Classroom is one of the core apps within Google G Suite for Education, and it is very much like existing learning management systems in use today. One of the premier benefits of Google Classroom is that it is free, and it works on iPads, Chromebooks, and countless other devices.

Google Classroom is most often used to create assignments, collect information, and offer feedback to students. It also has tools available like Stream, which is a communication channel for students and teachers that allows them to communicate efficiently, and it also will send assignment reminders to the students. Those who use Google Classroom can access and use all of the Google Suite Products, like Slides, Sheets, and Docs. Google Classroom is the hot trend in virtual learning because it offers many features that other services do not provide. The format of Google Classroom is easy to understand and easy to use, and Google is continually working on improving the platform.

Apple Classroom – This service is only available on Apple products, so it will only work on iOS devices, more specifically, the iPad. With its core features, the teacher can control the use of electronic devices in the classroom because there are limited types of devices the Apple Classroom is available on. Students can use any Mac screen or Apple TV to share their work with other students. And the limited accessibility will guarantee that all students will remain on the same webpage or app during the class period. Apple Classroom made its debut in 2016, and the company will freely admit that the platform is not a learning management system but more of an assistant for teachers. This platform gives teachers the ability to display the work of individual students for the entire class to see on the Apple function Airplay. Teachers have total control over the student's devices in the classroom, and they can turn them on or off as they please. They can also push websites and apps out to all of the iPads in the classroom and group the students in specific configurations for completing projects and other activities. From their iPad, the teacher can look into the iPad of each student to see what they are working on and what their progress is.

Apple Classroom is free for anyone to download, but the Classroom platform will need to be configured with a software management app designed for mobile devices before it will operate. The company is working on options that will allow teachers to add students to their software free of charge, and they are also working on document sharing options. Apple Classroom seems to work best for students in elementary school, since older students may quickly discover that putting their device into airplane mode makes it impossible for the teacher to know what they are doing.

Microsoft Classroom – This service is free with Office 365 Education and is compatible with Windows, iOS systems, Android devices, and any web browser. With the core features of the platform, teachers and students can chat through the communication channel. It is easier for students to work with each other online. Teachers can create assignments and share them with the students, and they can quickly provide feedback on the work the students are doing. Also released in 2016, it is the most recent release of the three big online classroom platforms. The platform is free for any school district or school that uses Office 365, and the platform works with OneNote Class Notebooks. It is a digital workspace where students can locate their assignments and share them with other students and with the teachers. They can also collaborate digitally with other students and receive feedback from the instructor.

The unique feature of Microsoft Classroom is that it has the ability to integrate with many different learning management systems, including Google Classroom. This will give the teacher additional abilities, such as sending grades to third-party gradebooks. Microsoft Classroom has many features that are similar to Google Classroom, like Conversation, which is like Google Stream and Microsoft Forms that lets teachers create and share quizzes and surveys quickly with their students.

There is also an available feature that allows the students to use a stylus to write notes directly into their documents. And with Microsoft Classroom, the teachers and students have direct access to all of the Office 365 tools like PowerPoint, Excel, and Word.

CORE FEATURES	GOOGLE	MICROSOFT	APPLE
The parent or guardian notification	Yes	No	No
Create assignments and distribute them	Yes	Yes	No
Post announcements and updates	Yes	Yes	Yes
Gradebook built-in	Yes	No	No
Monitor student devices	No	No	Yes
Save and store created documents in the Classroom	Yes	Yes	No
Data and content integration with 3rd party apps	Yes	Yes	No

Google Classroom is the frontrunner of the online classroom offerings from the big three companies.

The service is free for use and can be set up and learned in about an hour. Teachers can create and post assignments, quizzes, and other materials quickly. The Google Classroom app is the preferred online learning platform for many schools.

The Pros and Cons of Google Classroom

Google Classroom allows you to join millions of other online virtual learners in a classroom hub where you can communicate with your students, give them feedback on their progress whenever it is needed, and perfect the ability to share classroom assignments and documents. Google Classroom is the addition to online education that Google offered to the world to compensate for the lack of traditional in-class classroom instruction. There are definite pros and cons to the Google Classroom platform.

Advantages of Google Classroom

You can use Google Classroom even if you are not a regular user of Google and its services. Anyone will find using Google Classroom easy and fun. Since Google Classroom is delivered through the Google Chrome browser, it is accessible through all desktop computers, mobile phones, and portable tablets. It is relatively easy for users to add to as many students as they want. They can also create and save assignments and announcements in Google Docs, add links to other websites, attach files from Google Drive, and post videos from YouTube. The students will easily log in and access the features, as well as to receive their assignments and turn them in.

Google Docs is one of the best features of Google Classroom because the documents are saved online in the cloud, and they can be shared with an unlimited number of people. If you create an assignment or announcement in Google Docs and keep it in Google Drive, your students will then be able to access the document immediately. The documents that are saved in Google Drive are organized easily and can be divided into folders for easy storage and retrieval. You will not need to use emails to share information with your students. You will simply create a new document and then share that document with as many people as you want to share it with.

One quick click of the mouse will allow you to create an assignment and then share it with your students. With an equally easy one click of the mouse, your students can return the assignments to you. Google Classroom allows you to quickly check which students have already submitted their assignments and which students are still working on their work. It also allows you to offer feedback to the students immediately. The teacher also has the option of providing support online to the students. This makes your feedback more effective for your students because the remarks and comments are timely and relevant, and they will have a more significant impact on your student's ability to learn.

With Google Classroom, everything is done online, so there is no need to worry about printing and distributing paper copies of anything. And doing everything online eliminates the possibility that homework will be lost or destroyed accidentally. And the Google Classroom layout is user-friendly with its intuitive and straightforward design that Google users will already be familiar with. For many of the online courses, the teacher and students can make comments on the information that is being viewed while it is on the screen in the classroom. This allows the students to carry on a discussion with their classmates. The teacher can save the comments the students create and include them in links to add to future online discussions.

One of the best features of Google Classroom is the ability to set up a separate class for teachers and administrators to conduct seminars for professional development, share information in group meetings, and hold faculty meetings. This ability gives the educators the ability to share information and stay in touch, and the sessions can be recorded and shared later.

Disadvantages of Google Classroom

No system is perfect, and this also applies to Google Classroom. The platform is not able to be accessed across multiple domains. To log in to Google Classroom, you will need to be logged in to your Google Apps for Education email since the site can't be accessed from your personal email account. If you already own a personal email account through Google, then you might find it frustrating to juggle several email accounts. If you have a document or a photo in your personal email that you want to share in your classroom, then you will need to log into your personal email and save the item to the hard drive on your computer, and then log into your school account to share the article.

Some of the users who are not familiar with Google and its icons might become confused the first few times they use Google Classroom since many of the buttons and icons are specifically designed to look like they belong to Google. While there have been enhancements made to allow for easy sharing of YouTube videos on the Google Classroom site, the same enhancements have not been made for many other sites. This can make it difficult to share all of the items that you want to share with your students. And any existing documents will need to be converted into a structure that is compatible with Google Classroom. So a document that you have shared in Word will need to be converted into Google Docs so you can share it in your Google Classroom.

Anytime the teacher creates a document and shares it with their students, then the students become the owners of the document, which means they can make changes to the document whenever they want. They can also delete part or the entire document if they want. Even if this happens accidentally, it can still create problems. And the platform is not equipped with automatically generated quizzes for the students.

Frequently Asked Questions

Who can use the services of Google Classroom?

Schools that use Google G Suite for Education, those organizations that use Google G Suite for Nonprofits, and any individual who is over the age of 13, who has their own Google account.

Can Google Classroom be used by people with disabilities?

Google is continuously committed to improving the accessibility of Google Classroom for all users, but especially those who have learning disabilities. Those students who have visual impairments can use a screen reader for their computers or mobile devices. There are also Chrome extensions that are available for the computer. There is a text reader that will read the hard-to-read text, translate text, or simplify the vocabulary in the text. An add-on dictation tool comes equipped with predictive text that has smart spelling and grammar additions.

Is Google Classroom available on all devices?

Yes, it is available on android devices as well as chrome and iOS devices, with apps for tablets and phones.

What is the price for Google Classroom?

Google Classroom is free for all users.

Where does G Suite for Education connect with Google Classroom?

Google Classroom is a product that is available in G Suite for Education. G Suite also includes Google Drive, Slides, Sheets, and Docs. Google Classroom allows users to create classes, distribute and receive work, save documents, and stay organized.

Can I use Google Classroom with my students who have personal accounts if my school does not use G Suite for Education?

Unfortunately, the answer to that is no. To use Google Classroom with the students in the school, the school itself needs to start up a free account with G Suite for Education. Then the school will need to decide what features will be available for their teachers and students to use. And G Suite for Education offers additional security and privacy for students and teachers.

If Gmail is disabled on my G Suite for Education domain, am I still able to use Google Classroom?

Yes, you will still have access. Gmail does not need to be enabled for you to access and use Google Classroom. But is the administrator does not allow Gmail then the students and teachers will not receive any email notifications. The one discrepancy to this rule is if you have your email server set up to receive notifications from Google Drive, then you will be able to receive notifications from Google Classroom.

If Google Drive is disabled on my G Suite for Education domain, will I be able to use Google Classroom?

Since Google Classroom works with the G Suite for Education services like Google Docs and Google Drive, then Google Classroom will not work if Google Drive is disabled. If this happens, the other services like Google Docs will also be disabled, the teacher will not have the ability to attach the material to send to the students, and the features of Google Classroom will be minimal.

What is the difference between using Google Classroom with a personal account versus a school account?

Google Classroom us mostly the same platform for all users, but the users who have school accounts will have access to G Suite for Education services. The additional features available to them are the full administration of the user accounts and the ability to email summaries of student information to their guardians.

Does Google Classroom have ads in the content?

All Google G Suite for Education Services is entirely ad-free, and the data and content on the site are never used for any advertising purposes.

Who owns the content that is used in Google Classroom?

The school, teacher, and the students retain all ownership of their data and other material, so if they leave Google Classroom, they are free to take all of it with them. And the data and content will never be used for any purpose other than the meaning the school, teacher, and students use it for.

*How does my student find their work in Google
Classroom?*

When the student logs into Google Classroom, all
of the available classes will display on the screen
after the student sign is. Click on whichever class
you are looking for, then click on **Classwork** from
the top of the menu, and then click on **view my
work**.

*Can my student work on their assignments if they
do not have an internet connection?*

Students can work offline if they are working in
Google Slides, Sheets, or Docs in an android, iOS,
or Chrome application by making files available
offline under settings. In most cases, only the most
recently used documents will be available for
working offline, so it is better to utilize an internet
connection whenever it is possible.

How do I keep track of my child's work in their online classes?

The parent or guardian can ask to receive updates by email regarding the work and progress students are doing in Google Classroom. They can receive weekly or even daily updates. The teacher or the domain administrator can add the parent or guardian email address to Google Classroom so they can receive regular updates. The administrator of the domain must first enable the feature, and then the class teacher must add the guardian's email address.

Chapter 5: Recent Enhancements

Google is continuously working to upgrade and enhance the features of Google Classroom. Many of the upgrades that have already been made were suggested by current users who thought of a better way to run the classroom. New upgrades and enhancements include several user-friendly changes.

Originality Report

With Originality Reports, the teachers and students can check their work for authenticity, i.e., plagiarism. When the Originality Report is run, it will compare the work of the student in the Google Docs file against books and webpages on the Internet. The resulting report will show any links to sources that are detected and will also flag any text that is not cited by the student author. Currently, the Originality Report is only available for the Google G Suite accounts that are set to

English, Swedish, Spanish, Portuguese, Norwegian, Italian, and Indonesian. If you are using a Google G Suite for Education account, you can activate the Originality Report to scan three assignments for each class. If the administrator upgrades the account to G Suit Enterprise for Education, you will have access to unlimited Originality Reports.

Teachers and students can view a report for forty-five days, and after that, you will need to run another report. When the teacher turns on the reports for any assignment, the student can run up to three reports on their submission before they turn the work into the teacher. The teacher can't see the reports that the students run. After the student runs the third report, they will be able to continue working on the submission before they turn it into the teacher.

When either teachers or students use the originality reports, Google does not save the content that is submitted in the report. Google also does not assume any ownership pf the content. The content belongs to the teacher or the student; whoever is the original owner of the report. The report will only search for content that is available publicly on the internet and the reports are never stored permanently.

Student Information Systems (SIS)

Teachers who use Google Classroom can now export the grades of the students directly into their student information system (SIS). Currently, this feature is only available for Infinite Campus, although more partnership agreements are currently in development. The administration of the school will need to set up the connection, and then the teachers can link the classes and then export the student's grades.

Tech Toolkit for Families and Guardians of Students

The learning and well-being of a child are greatly enhanced when educators and the parents or guardians of the child can connect in meaningful ways. The most significant piece of communication is giving the parents and guardians of the students the ability to know about and understand what the student is doing in the classroom. The parents must support the needs of the student at home, and to do so, they will need to understand the technology that runs the Google Classroom site. Since Google provides much of this technology, they want the parents to be able to understand it. And while they want the parents and guardians to be able to understand the technology their students are using, it is nearly impossible to find the time and resources to act in a technical support capacity. Google created a Tech Toolkit for Families and Guardians that will help build a better relationship between educators and their families by providing resources and training to the families of the students. This will help to establish a better overall connection that will allow the students to keep learning and growing. The quick training videos help to explain the tools that Google Classroom uses and helpful tips for the parents and guardians. The kit includes A series of videos titled Google for Education, a glossary of Google terms, a list of best practices to enhance family engagement and a frequently asked question segment geared around technical knowledge of Google Classroom.

Google Meet

Users of Google G Suite Enterprise for Education have access to Google Meet, which your organization or school can use for class meetings online. If you are using Google Classroom, every class will have the link for the dedicated meetings that students and teachers can use to join meetings in Google Classroom. Users of G Suite for Education will activate the permission to create and join the video meetings in their email account.

The teacher owns the meeting calendar and is the one who creates the meeting. This means the teacher is the only one who can remove participants or mute them. If a participant is removed by the teacher for any reason, they will not be able to rejoin that video meeting. Those participants will not be allowed back until the teacher invites them back to the next meeting. The teacher has the power to view, approve, and deny any external requests to join a video meeting. Any participant who has already been denied entry twice for any reason will not be allowed to request permission to join any video meeting. The teacher can also decide whether or not participants can share their screens with others during the meeting, and if the participants can send chat messages to other participants during the meeting.

If necessary, to improve the quality of the video, the participants can turn off their individual cameras and display their profile pictures. If the audio for the meeting is of poor quality, the participants can use their phones for the audio feed instead. If the class is larger, the teacher can create a live stream event in place of using an interactive video for the class meeting. The lesson can be recorded for sharing later. Questions can be accepted from the participants and displayed in Google Slides, to help keep the students engaged and participating. The teacher can enable live captions for the students who are hard of hearing or deaf.

Teacher Center

The Google Classroom Teacher Center provides access to online training that is free for teachers to help them use the most popular tools that Google offers. The training center provides teachers three separate sections for training with Google Classroom. The Training page will show all of the training courses that are available for teachers who are new to Google Classroom. The course in Fundamentals will get new teachers started in the technical knowledge they need for Google Classroom. If you already have familiarity with the technology in Google Classroom, then you should start with the advanced course, which will give you a more in-depth knowledge of Google Classroom and all that it offers.

The next part of the teacher training is the training for the Devices. This will give teachers a good understanding of the functions of Google Classroom on Android tablets and Chromebooks. And the last part of the teacher training is the course that shows the teachers different ways to be competent teachers in Google Classroom.

If you are planning to conduct virtual teaching in an online capacity, Google Classroom is the site you need to be a successful teacher who turns out successful students. The technology that is available to you will make your days in the virtual classroom enjoyable. Google Classroom is the platform that you need to create a successful teaching environment for you and your students.

Conclusion

Thank you for making it through to the end of *Google Classroom for Teachers: The Complete Step-By-Step Illustrated Guide for Teachers on How to Teach Using Google Classroom and to Benefit From Virtual Learning*, let's hope it was informative and able to provide you with all of the tools you need to achieve your goals whatever they may be.

The next step is to use the guidance that you received in this book and start setting up your own version of Google Classroom. You will definitely want to take advantage of all of the technical aspects of Google Classrooms. Nut ultimately this will be your version of Google Classroom. As the teacher you will be the one who sets up the classes on Google Classroom and decides the content of those classes. You will be the one to add on the roster of students and make the classes available for your students.

You see in this book just how easy it is to get started in Google Classroom. Setting up the entire site probably will not take you more than two or three hours at eh most. When you have the students added and the basic templates set up for your classes, then you will be ready to add content and invite your students in to begin classes. You will be able to make announcements to the students and assign projects and tasks to them. You can assemble a calendar and set events on it, and then you can share that calendar with your students. You can set up video conferences with your students, share pictures for them to see, and link into other sites that will assist you in imparting knowledge to your students. Everything you need to know to do all of this is found in this book.

Keep this book with you and use it as your guide to success. And finally, if you found this book useful in any way, a review on Amazon is always appreciated!

www.ingramcontent.com/pod-product-compliance
Lightning Source LLC
Chambersburg PA
CBHW051106050726
47592CB00002B/699